Electronic Marketing

Emerging TV and Computer Channels for Interactive Home Shopping

by Lawrence Strauss

Knowledge Industry Publications, Inc.
White Plains, NY and London

Communications Library

Electronic Marketing: Emerging TV and Computer
Channels for Interactive Home Shopping

Library of Congress Cataloging in Publication Data
Strauss, Lawrence.
  Electronic marketing.

  (Communications library)
  Bibliography: p.
  Includes index.
  1. Electronic marketing. I. Title. II. Series.
HF5415.122.S77 1983   381'.1   83-185
ISBN 0-86729-023-4

Printed in the United States of America

10 9 8 7 6 5 4 3 2 1

Table of Contents

List of Tables and Figures

List of Illustrations

Introduction

Shopping via computer and television is, for most of us, a fanciful notion reserved for the future. But to others—a small yet growing number—it represents a significant development that is both serious and close at hand. Innovations spawned by technology often have a way of being dismissed as impractical for consumer application. It took ten years for credit cards to catch on and about the same amount of time for automatic teller machines to become widely accepted. As recently as five years ago, pay TV and video cassettes for home use didn't appear to be the sure winners they are today. Video games and personal computers are the latest examples of consumer products that emerge and engulf us in quite unexpected ways.

The use of electronics for buying and selling goods and services actually goes back to the 1920s, when sponsors started using radio to persuade listeners to buy their products. In the late 1940s, consumer electronics took a leap forward with the introduction of television. With its visual dimension, television had decided advantages over radio for electronic marketing. Marketers of a wide range of products and services quickly adopted television as the primary advertising vehicle for reaching mass audiences and gave it an increasing proportion of advertising budgets that had previously been invested in radio, magazines and newspapers.

In the late 1970s, a new cluster of media components began to appear that were to revolutionize television itself—the new electronic media (NEM). Cable TV, satellite communications, video cassettes, video discs and personal computers all became widely accessible to the consumer market. At the same time, advances in microprocessors and communications made it technically possible to convert any TV set into a computer-like terminal capable of two-way transmissions controlled by the viewer. Prestel in Britain and Qube in Columbus, OH, emerged as primitive forerunners of two-way TV systems that can transform passive viewing into active participation. The impact of the new electronic media is already widely reflected in the home entertainment field. Pay TV, video cassettes and video games are attracting increasing numbers of viewers and, as a result, are throwing the conventional programming strategies of the major networks into disarray.

The new electronic media, however, can be used for much more than entertainment. Shopping, banking, electronic mail, education and information retrieval are all possible using "smart" home terminals connected by cable or telephone lines to remote data bases. Thus, the stage is set for a vast expansion of electronic marketing. The technology exists, and it is rapidly improving. Although the costs of electronic marketing are still high, they are bound to drop as technological innovations continue and as the costs are spread over other electronic services offered to the consumer.

Three important forces will accelerate the acceptance of electronic marketing. First, the business community, seeking ways to improve productivity, to enter new markets and to stay competitive, will increasingly support new technology as a way of achieving these goals. In doing so, it will encourage the use of self-service systems that eliminate middle levels of distribution. Second, direct marketing, which already relies on computers and advanced communications, is finding that the interactive features of the new technologies work very effectively in reaching targeted audiences. Third, an increasingly "computer literate" society is willing to use technology to save time and money, to eliminate the drugery of routine shopping and to find information about goods and services.

In the "information age," the past is of limited value in predicting the future. Most of us think in universal terms when we look to the future. For example, three of the most influential innovations of the past 100 years—telephone, radio and television—are available in practically every household. Will the new services including electronic marketing have to become universal if they are to become successful? Absolutely not.

Electronic marketing and its companion services will develop along segmented lines. By the early 1990s, the proportion of homes capable of conducting two-way, viewer-controlled dialogs will not exceed 30% of all households. However, the crucial factors will be the demographics of the households and the intensity of use, not the overall size of the audience.

Furthermore, development will not proceed in a linear fashion. As John Naisbitt states in his recent best-seller, *Megatrends,* "The gee-whiz futurists are always wrong because they believe technological innovation travels in a straight line. It doesn't. It weaves and bobs and lurches and sputters."[1]

How pervasive electronic marketing becomes is anyone's guess. The total demise of retail stores, real estate agencies and travel bureaus is nowhere in sight. Yet who could have predicted ten years ago that a significant percentage of the TV-viewing population would be playing a game

---

[1]John Naisbitt, *Megatrends: Ten New Directions Transforming Our Lives* (New York, NY: Warner Books, Inc., 1982), p. 41.

called Pac-Man or paying to watch movies and sport events that had always been available on "free" TV? Shopping by computer for apparel, groceries, vacation trips or insurance may not create the excitement of playing a video game. But for many of us it certainly beats the day-to-day hassle of dealing with an increasingly unresponsive retail system.

The only thing that seems certain is the uncertainty of what the future holds in store. Based on what is known today, more changes can be expected in the communications field over the next 10 years than in the past 40, and more sophisticated forms of electronic marketing will figure prominently in those changes.

This book examines a number of key elements that are crucial to the development of electronic marketing over the next decade, such as the communications support structure that is evolving; the key players involved in the race for strategic market shares; the trials that are being conducted and that will form the basis for commercial services by the mid-to-late 1980s; the affinity between direct marketing and new technology; the prospects for widespread consumer acceptance; the economic and sociological hurdles that face both users and service providers; and the role that advertising will play in the creation of new distribution systems.

1

The Development of Electronic Marketing

INTRODUCTION

The year is 2000. Most homes are equipped with large screen projection TVs providing stereophonic sound and picture resolution of extraordinary quality based on high definition television technology. This equipment is located in the household "entertainment center" along with audio equipment and video peripherals which perform a variety of functions using software from both internal and external sources.

Homes are also equipped with video terminals that can be connected to the entertainment system, or used to retrieve information and conduct transactions. The cost of computing power and the size of microprocessors are a fraction of what they were in the 1980s and 1990s, and personal computing capability is pervasive.

Computer Teleshopping

This computing power makes "telecommunications merchandising" possible on a wide scale. The computer takes charge of a variety of shopping chores. It handles most routine "teleshopping" completely on its own, by ordering basic foods and household products on a regular schedule based on usage patterns and consumption rates. The computer scans product information banks and then makes purchasing decisions; these information banks have largely replaced sponsored commercials which had been favored for so long by advertisers to carry messages to consumers.

In addition to handling routine shopping, the computer continuously searches the data bases of merchants and service providers for special offers, bargains or unusual items. The search routines are established based on specific user preferences. Such preferences range from traveling to far-off, exotic locations to things much more mundane, such as ordering particular items of clothing. Moreover, programs can be changed at any time, as individual moods, tastes and predilections change.

The search routines are carried out by the computer, day and night, seven days a week, throughout the year. When a usable item is identified, the information is made available on a small, inexpensive printer or is called up from computer memory by the user, who has been alerted to its availability.

For shopping not covered by the automatic routines, the user can intervene to gather as little or as much information as is needed and to place an order. Electronic shoppers switch back and forth from text and graphic material to segments with moving video and sound for product demonstrations, travelogs or other descriptive material. This capability is referred to as "video on demand," and it is based on advanced video disc technology combined with high-speed computers. In most cases direct consumer dialogs with vendor data bases are possible using an advanced videotext system as a "gateway," or switch, to access computers outside the host network.

When an order is placed, payment is arranged using a credit card, debit card or "smart card" (a device the size of a credit card, which incorporates a tiny microprocessor and which can be used for making payments from a remote terminal). Banks, using highly advanced electronic funds transfer procedures, coordinate with merchandising and service organizations to provide a totally integrated electronic services network.

For transactions involving the physical movement of goods, delivery or pickup instructions are relayed to the vendor. For services involving travel or entertainment, an electronic "ticket" can be transmitted using the home printer. The system can even deliver coupons ("viewpons") to people at home either on demand or automatically. Of course, the possibilities for junk video mail are almost endless, but the user will be able to pick and choose what it is he wants sent, based on personal preferences.

Some consumers will rely heavily on electronic marketing methods; others will continue to shop in the traditional way. Obviously there is a continuum based on personal preferences and motivations, but people will be able to move back and forth on the continuum. In some cases, consumers will be obligated to use the new methods because certain dealers and service providers, as we know them, either will have disappeared or will have been forced to adopt electronic distribution practices for economic and social reasons, thus leaving the consumer little choice in the matter of how he obtains goods and services.

Truth or Science Fiction

Is all of this a realistic scenario for the future or is it the harebrained scheme of futurists and technologists? Predicting precisely the technological environment at the turn of the century is not practical, and it is certainly not the objective of this book.

However, as the futurists ply their craft, technology is racing ahead, and it is interacting with significant economic, political and social forces. Although the results are far from certain, the major trends can be discerned, and they point to revolutionary changes in the way goods and services are exchanged. The technology that drives these changes is powerful, but it is less important than the implications for consumers, business organizations and society as a whole.

Webster's *New World Dictionary* defines marketing as "all business activity involved in the moving of goods from the producer to the consumer, including selling, advertising, packaging, etc." Marketing expert Philip Kotler defines it even more broadly when he says, "marketing is human activity directed at satisfying needs and wants through exchange processes."[1] Electronic marketing will not change these basic definitions, but it will provide new tools to get the job done. These tools will be made possible by high-speed computers, advanced communications and video display techniques that will be easy to use and available at a cost affordable to the mass market. Increasing reliance on technology will revolutionize the structure of marketing for both buyers and sellers in ways we can hardly imagine.

THE NEW ELECTRONIC MEDIA

The 1980s are witness to the "new electronic media" (NEM), an eclectic term referring to a wide range of hardware and software made possible by technology, which is revolutionizing communications and transaction channels (broadcasting, publishing, advertising, entertainment, banking, shopping, information retrieval, telecommunications and data processing). Examples of the NEM include: cable and pay TV, video cassettes, video discs, video games and personal computers. Future developments will include dramatic innovations such as direct broadcast satellites and high definition television.

The NEM promise gold at the end of the rainbow, and big money is taking part in the search for possible rewards. Worldwide investment in videotext technology is steadily increasing. The search is led by telephone companies, cable TV operators, broadcasters, publishers, financial service organizations, electronic hardware manufacturers, data processing vendors and many others. The new technology will make it possible for many

---

[1]Philip Kotler, *Marketing Management: Analysis, Planning and Control,* 3d ed. (Englewood Cliffs, NJ: Prentice Hall, 1976).

of these organizations to enter markets that were never before accessible to them.

Entertainment Services

The impact of the NEM has so far been greatest in the distribution of entertainment to the home market. By the end of 1982, basic cable penetration had reached 32% of all U.S. households. The rapid growth in pay TV services, whether transmitted by cable or over the air, proves quite convincingly that large numbers of people are willing to pay $10 a month or more to watch unedited motion pictures without commercial interruption in the comfort of their own homes. By the beginning of October 1982, pay cable subscriptions had reached 18.3 million and were growing at a faster rate than basic cable subscriptions. Subscription TV (STV) and multipoint distribution services (MDS) were reaching an additional 2.3 million homes.

Viewers who elect to watch prerecorded programs or want to "time-shift" their favorite TV programs are purchasing video cassette recorders (VCRs). VCR owner population as of October 1, 1982 was 4.5 million and is expected to reach 14% of all U.S. homes by the end of 1985.[2] This emerging hardware/software package liberates the viewer from the absolute control over schedules and programming that has always been exercised by the networks.

The home entertainment industry in the U.S. has been built on advertiser-supported broadcast television. The key to success has been the ability to attract mass audiences. The new electronic media are causing the mass audience to fragment, as viewers are offered more and more options. As audiences are increasingly diverted from traditional viewing, mass advertising is losing its efficiency. It is quite clear that, as this happens, advertisers will have to implement new strategies to offset declining efficiency.

Non-entertainment Services

Significant changes in the distribution of entertainment seem certain. However, the outlook for non-entertainment services is less certain: consumer demand is unknown, and consumer acceptance of using computers and computer-like services is unknown. Much of the same technology that delivers entertainment services to the home today is capable of providing a wide variety of non-entertainment applications including home security, energy management, medical alert, shopping, banking, electronic mail and

---

[2]*Home Video and Cable Report* (October 25, 1982).

educational programs. This delivery system could also provide electronically published information such as classified advertising, Yellow Pages, travel and entertainment listings, catalogs and directories.

Cable television and the telephone system could each become the backbone of the delivery system for such services. Broadcast television could also be used, but to a lesser extent. The cable and telephone industries have not coordinated their developmental activities, largely due to the former's fear of an unregulated AT&T as a competitor. However, economics could drive them together through the development of hybrid systems, which combine both systems for interactive service. "Downstream" cable and "upstream" telephone links are less costly to install than two-way coaxial cable.

Electronic marketing made its appearance in a primitive form in the early days of radio, tied to commercials that solicited direct responses from listeners. However, commercials run in such fashion were really "one-way" since immediate response was not possible. The age of "two-way" electronic marketing dawned when radio or television was linked to the telephone. The result was the direct response commercial designed to elicit immediate inquiries or orders. As we show in Chapter 3, direct response is the forerunner of the next wave of electronic marketing, which will enable consumers to communicate interactively with merchants and service providers. An important distinction between earlier forms of electronic marketing and what can be expected in the future is that future dialogs will often be initiated by the buyer rather than the seller. Consumers employing advanced computer technology will search out products and services to suit specific needs, although in many cases these needs will have been stimulated by advertising messages directed to them.

Television provided direct marketers with a new tool to be used alongside conventional techniques, such as direct mail, catalogs, newspaper supplements, coupons and the telephone. Cable TV opens up many new possibilities for enhancing direct response TV commercials. It also provides marketers with the ability to establish fully interactive systems that will allow consumers to communicate directly with merchants and service providers on a real-time basis. When this happens, a transformation in shopping habits and in supplier strategies will take place. The age of electronic marketing truly will have arrived.

Cable TV

Cable TV has been available in the U.S. for over 30 years; so it is not really a new media form. However, over the past five years it has begun to offer new sources of programming for TV viewers: pay TV supported by subscription fees, and special-interest programming supported by a combination of advertising and cable operator payments. (See Chapter 4.) Cable advertising revenues could reach $200 million in 1982, compared to an anticipated $14 billion for broadcast TV. Although cable ad revenues are expected to grow substantially by 1990 (estimates run from $2 to $3 billion), they will still be only a small percentage of the overall advertising universe, which could reach $145 to $150 billion by that time.[3]

Advertising on cable closely resembles advertising on broadcast television. Cable also has drawn its share of direct response ads, which are used in much the same way as they are on broadcast television and radio. However, cable offers the possibility of employing advertising and promotional techniques to support electronic marketing that have not been used in other media. Conventional ads can be tailored to blend with the programming to produce "hybrids" referred to as advertorials, infomercials or documercials. Hybrids have been shunned by broadcast TV because of FCC restrictions on time, and considerations of fairness and equal time which do not apply to cable. Shopping channel formats can be developed whereby a full channel is devoted to product promotion; and cable's full channel capability can be used for teletext or videotext. These unique applications are expected to become important sources of revenue for cable, and the amount of advertising dollars generated could eventually exceed "conventional" cable advertising dollars.

Videotext

Videotext is a two-way communications system that provides text and graphics by linking a computerized data base to low-cost video terminals via cable and/or telephone lines. (See Figure 1.1.) The objective of videotext designers is quite simple: to provide economical and easy-to-use computerized time sharing with a wide range of applications for the mass market. Since videotext offers interactive capability, it can be used for shopping, banking, information retrieval and electronic mail. (See Chapter 5 for further discussion of videotext and Table 1.A for information on U.S. videotext and teletext services.)

Times Mirror Videotex Services is one of several trials that provides a wide range of interactive services to people at home. In addition to news, information and games, it offers electronic mail by which individuals can send messages to each other including "Hallmark video greetings"; tele-

---

[3]1990 estimate by author based on figures supplied by Robert Coen, McCann-Erickson, Inc., of $67.9 billion in total U.S. advertising revenues up to 1982 and assuming a 12% annual increase each year thereafter.

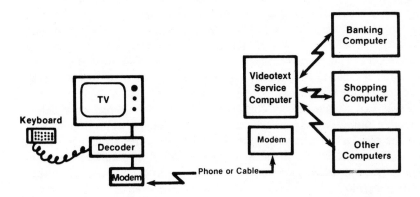

Figure 1.1:   A Typical Videotext System

Source: "What is Videotex?" Copyright © 1982 Times Mirror Videotex Services, Inc. Reprinted by permission.

shopping from Sears, local retailers or through Comp-U-Store, an electronic data base shopping service (see Chapter 5); tickets to sports and entertainment events through Ticketron; access to flight schedules through the Official Airlines Guide; and home banking service through the Bank of America.

Three components are necessary to provide videotext service: a network operator, usually a cable or telephone company; information providers, such as publishers, service organizations, retailers and banks; and hardware suppliers, who provide equipment for the network operators and system users.

The British Post Office (now British Telecom) introduced Prestel, the world's first commercial videotext service, in 1979 for home and business use. The service uses the telephone system to deliver information to subscribers with specially equipped TV sets. At the end of 1982 Prestel was reporting about 20,000 subscribers, and 90% of them were business users. In Prestel, text and graphic material is created, using special equipment, and stored in a computerized data base. A user can call up "frames" or pages which can be displayed on many types of video terminals, such as a specially adapted TV, a standard data terminal, a personal computer or a communicating word processor.

Pages are displayed on an ordinary TV screen in color using text and low resolution graphics. Some displays are 40 x 24 characters and others are 40 x 20 characters. Eventually, when uniform standards are adopted, they could be reduced to 32 x 16 characters to make reading them as easy as possible. Visual displays of this type provide much less information than a typewritten page, a newspaper or magazine page or a computer display used for business purposes.

Pages can be selected by consulting a "menu" or directory which is available online and sometimes in printed form, as well. Getting to a specific piece of information involves following a tree-structured search procedure, or in some cases, using keywords. A tree-structured search procedure is a hierarchical approach to retrieving information. Users move from generalized to specific data on a step-by-step basis, selecting a "branch" at each step. This is a much simpler and easier-to-understand approach than keyword search, and it requires the least expensive type of equipment to perform. (See Figure 1.2.)

Videotext opens up many new possibilities for electronic marketing. The user is able to communicate directly with computerized catalogs or directories, which can be continuously changed to reflect the most up-to-the-minute conditions on prices, inventories, promotions and other information. Information and service providers (retailers, banks, publishers, travel organizations etc.) can create new pages and revise existing ones through computer terminals specially designed for text and graphic material. Terminals can be located in homes, offices or even public locations.

The computer capability of videotext gives the user the ability to sort, compare and cross-reference great quantities of information in a way that would be impossible or very difficult without computer assistance. For example, a buyer might be interested in knowing where a certain item was available, and he might want to compare prices. Further, he might want to request information on performance, operating costs, service policies and warranties. This information can be stored in the system for review by a potential buyer so that all the research on a particular purchase can be completed before the consumer makes his purchasing decision. After completing his research, he may place an order, request additional information or make a personal visit to a merchant or service provider. Figures 1.3 and 1.4 illustrate teleshopping possibilities on the Canadian Telidon videotext system.

Teletext

Teletext is a one-way communication system that transmits text and graphics to specially adapted TV sets by broadcast or cable. Like videotext, teletext was pioneered in Great Britain where the British Broadcasting Corporation (BBC) launched its Ceefax system in 1976. This system was

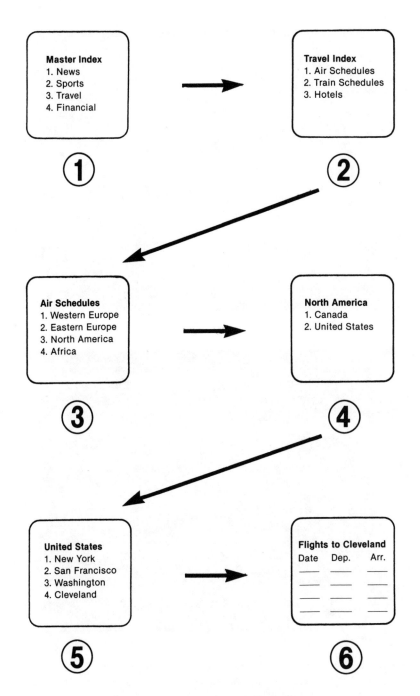

**Figure 1.2 A Tree-Search Procedure:
Locating Information on Flights to Cleveland**

Figure 1.3 Telidon videotext system provides a picture of the performer and ticket prices, as well as a seating plan of the theater. Courtesy Telidon Videotex Systems Inc.

Figure 1.4 The shopper can choose from among different types of merchandise. Special prices are advertised for particular products. Courtesy Telidon Videotex Systems Inc.

soon followed by Oracle, offered by the BBC's commercial counterpart, the Independent Broadcasting Authority (IBA). By the end of 1982, teletext service in Great Britain was attracting 25,000 new subscribers each month, and over 500,000 subscribers (estimated) were expected to be using it by the end of 1982.

A teletext subscriber is supplied with a decoder (attached to or built into the set), and a small keypad that enables him to "grab" an individual page for viewing as it cycles by. The waiting time for the desired page is usually just a few seconds. Broadcast teletext is piggybacked on the vertical blanking interval (VBI), the unused portion of a TV signal, and there is a severe limit on the number of pages that can be transmitted (usually about 100). Cable teletext uses full channel transmission, enabling several thousand pages to be stored and sent to subscribers.

Despite the obvious limitations of broadcast teletext, it could be one of the first of the new media to be introduced on a widespread basis. The reason is that it can be added onto existing facilities at relatively low cost. A number of trials have been or are being conducted by broadcasters in the U.S. (see Chapter 4 and Table 1.A). Broadcast teletext is an informational rather than a transactional medium. It can be regarded as an electronic newspaper that specializes in highly perishable information that changes frequently, such as: news bulletins, weather reports, road conditions, sports scores, stock prices and travel information. Broadcast teletext is the type of service that viewers are likely to consult for quick reference rather than in-depth information.

However, both teletext modes are expected to attract advertising support, and they could be used for certain types of electronic marketing. The big problem with any kind of teletext for the foreseeable future is at the receiving end. Until low cost decoders can be supplied, and can be attached to a sufficient number of sets, the teletext audience will not be large enough to attract much advertising support. The classic chicken-and-egg syndrome is hobbling the early application of new media to electronic marketing.

Video Discs

An array of hardware devices is becoming available which could boost electronic marketing activities. One of the most promising devices to appear so far is the video disc, which resembles an LP record, and can store vast amounts of information that can be played back through an ordinary TV. Information on the optical disc can be accessed randomly and displayed as a still picture or as a continuous presentation with text, graphics, moving video and sound. It is an electronic catalog in every sense, and it allows the viewer to refer instantaneously to any one of thousands of pages.

Some companies have already experimented with video disc catalogs. General Motors purchased 10,000 and Ford purchased 4200 of the optical type for use in dealer training and sales presentations. In 1981, Sears ran a trial using a video disc catalog in both home and showroom settings (see Chapter 6 for further details). Cosmetics giant Avon also tested discs for a video network to teach its sales force about new products and sales techniques. However, early in 1983, Avon decided to purchase cassette equipment which was preferred by the sales representatives.

Despite its obvious potential, the video disc is not destined to be used widely in electronic marketing for a number of years, for two reasons. First, the players have not sold well and thus the player population will remain very limited until sales pick up dramatically, an event that is not expected for some time. As of late 1982, there were approximately 300,000 players in the field, and this figure includes a high percentage of the RCA version, which is not suitable for electronic catalogs since it does not have interactive capability.[4] Until a substantially greater number of interactive players reaches consumers, publishing of electronic catalogs will not be economically justified.

Second, there is an inherent technological problem. Within the current state of the art, a video disc cannot be erased or changed, which means that once an electronic catalog is produced, it cannot be updated. This limitation also applies to printed catalogs, but since videotext and teletext can be continuously updated, video discs are at an obvious disadvantage. The ideal system would feed changes to a video disc that could be updated on a regular basis, but such a development is many years away. Such a system would combine the high-level visual presentation of the video disc with the real-time features of teletext and videotext. However, for the foreseeable future, electronic marketing applications of the video disc will be limited to in-store point-of-sale use and catalog showroom demonstrations.

Video Cassettes

Video cassettes could also play a role in electronic marketing, albeit a minor one. Prerecorded video tapes with short commercial segments are one possibility. However, viewers could easily reject these commercials by fast-forwarding right on by them. One of the reasons that prerecorded video cassettes have become as popular as they have is that they are commercial free.

A more likely possibility is prerecorded promotional or demonstration tapes that provide viewers with information in an entertaining way. Any-

---

[4]*Home Video and Cable Report* (October 25, 1982).

thing from sports equipment to major appliances could be the focus of prerecorded video cassettes, which could be purchased, but, more likely, rented by people with an interest in doing some prebuying research. Existing customers might receive such material free of charge, much like catalogs are distributed. The same policy might be applied for those customers identified as top prospects.

The video cassette player population could be large enough in a year or two to consider such an approach. In the long run, the interactive video disc will become the favored medium for electronic catalogs. Its interactive capability is superior to the video cassette since it performs more like a book, where specific sections can be quickly accessed. However, the video cassette could find a niche for promotional material, available on request or provided unsolicited to prospective customers.

Personal Computers

Personal computers are also becoming an increasingly important part of the picture. Some of the home banking services that are being developed depend upon personal computers linked to telephone lines, while others are based on specially adapted TV sets. The former approach emphasizes segmentation while the latter is built on the mass market concept visualized by videotext promoters.

Despite the cost of personal computers, they are currently a hot selling item in an otherwise recessionary economy. Even though the population of personal computers in U.S. households will be tiny compared to that of TV sets for many years to come, the users of personal computers, by their dedication to technology, represent a small but growing nucleus of consumers who will take advantage of all types of interactive services, from games to shopping. The behavior of this group will be crucial to the long-term development and acceptance of electronic transactions.

STATUS OF ELECTRONIC TRANSACTIONS

The promotion of new electronic media has differed widely from country to country. This uneven approach is bound to affect the timetable for putting applications into practice. In Western Europe, Canada and Japan, where national governments generally control all or part of the broadcast media, videotext and teletext have been heavily supported through direct government subsidies. France, Canada and Britain have competed fiercely for overseas markets to sell their new technologies. Domestic markets in those countries are not large enough to justify the huge up-front research, development and promotional costs required to launch the new technologies. The early leads gained by other countries would seem to place them ahead of the U.S. in the race to set up electronic marketing systems. West Germany's Bildschirmtext system, which uses certain elements of Prestel technology, appears closest to establishing a commercial system that offers electronic marketing and banking. France is not too far behind, and England, which was first to offer commercial service, has a lot of catching up to do, since it left transactional capability out of the original Prestel design.

In the U.S., the government has not been involved and developments have been quite different. Since the late 1970s, cable TV has expanded rapidly, bringing pay TV with it, and the video disc has been introduced. Both will eventually play a role in the development of electronic marketing, but the impetus behind their development is mostly entertainment. In the U.S., videotext and teletext have not moved beyond the trial stage. They so far have not gained the attention that they have attracted in Canada, Britain, France and West Germany.

The U.S. scene clearly reflects many fundamental problems that afflict the communication business: uncertainty over the future of AT&T (made somewhat clearer in January 1982 with the Justice Department's settlement); lack of agreement among newspapers and broadcasters concerning long-term implications of the new electronic media; and reluctance by cable operators and hardware manufacturers to make substantial investments early in the game.

Thus, the U.S. is still very much in the trial stage. Publishers, broadcasters, computer manufacturers, common carriers, retailers, banks, travel organizations and direct marketers are all interested, and some are beginning to step up their investments in the new technologies. At the present time the banking industry seems to have forged far ahead. At least a dozen banks throughout the nation are pouring millions into the development of home banking systems. The otherwise conservative industry is a major catalyst for change, and home banking could be as significant an introduction as earlier innovations dependent upon technology such as credit cards, electronic funds transfer and automatic teller machines. Interestingly, however, these earlier innovations took at least ten years before they were widely accepted. However, with the banking industry undergoing fundamental restructuring, widespread application of home banking will probably not take a decade to catch on.

Public Acceptance of New Technologies

When radio and television were introduced, they represented new technologies that were nothing short of revolutionary. For the first time in history, sound, and later pictures and sound, could be transmitted over the air and received simultaneously in millions of homes throughout the world. Within 20 years of their introduction, radio and television were to be as universally accepted as the telephone, which had made its appearance in the previous century.

Ironically, these inventions were not originally welcomed by the public, whose acceptance of new technologies has always been hesitant at first. The historical lesson of the telephone, radio and TV is that they were originally viewed with skepticism, if not downright ridicule.

For example, when the telephone was first introduced in England, many people felt that it added little to what messenger or postal service could perform. In the beginning, radio's major use was by newspapers and hotels for promotional purposes. The first commercial radio station was KDKA, established in Pittsburgh by Westinghouse. The year was 1920, and by setting up a station, Westinghouse had a way to encourage people to buy one of its newest products, the radio set. In the early years of radio, it took a vivid imagination to predict where the medium would eventually go. When television was first introduced, it was used as "visual radio" with actors doing stiff, visual renditions of radio dramas.[5]

In time, radio and television were to broaden their appeal, and by doing so, they became something quite different from what they had started out to be. Radio started out serving local communities much as newspapers did. In time, however, it expanded its coverage by establishing networks which spanned the nation. It became a mass entertainment medium which rivaled the motion picture industry, which really wasn't much older than radio. Radio's preeminence as a mass medium was seriously challenged with the introduction of television, but in a Darwinian sense it was to evolve into its current form as a "narrowcast" vehicle specializing in news, music and talk shows delivered both locally and on a network basis.

Television moved from its limited programming formats to become the replacement for radio as a mass entertainment vehicle. It has also become a major source of news, a development that has contributed to the demise of many of the nation's newspapers. Cable television originated as a transmission system to carry TV signals to remote areas where reception was otherwise poor or nonexistent. Today, it is evolving on its own, offering alternatives to broadcast TV. These alternatives include a wide range of specialized programming, from movies and sports to weather and health.

Video cassette equipment has been used by TV broadcasters going back to the 1950s. Half-inch video cassette equipment for home use was intro-

---

[5]For details on the early history of radio and TV, the author is indebted to Lawrence Bergreen, *Look Now Pay Later: The Rise of Network Broadcasting* (New York: Doubleday, 1980).

troduced by Sony in 1975 as a means to tape TV programs off-air for later playback, thus providing program "time-shift" capability. Prerecorded programming for use on such equipment was an afterthought, but today, the sale and rental of prerecorded video tapes has caught on in a big way. These examples all indicate that new technologies usually evolve to offer new services for which they were not necessarily intended when they were introduced. The major question today is when and to what extent will the new electronic media evolve to offer non-entertainment services that consumers perceive as useful.

Public Acceptance of Electronic Marketing

The new electronic media are going through many of the same developmental problems that afflicted earlier technologies as they search for new applications. In theory, many of the services that can be delivered to the home have the potential to provide real benefits. Electronic newspapers, classified advertising and Yellow Pages, banking, shopping and electronic mail all have inherent appeal, but they must overcome substantial economic and psychological barriers. Not only must the new applications be developed, but they must be sold to the public as benefits worth paying for and adjusting to.

Economic considerations are of paramount importance for the development of the new electronic media. For the more advanced technologies, such as videotext, to be applied to teleshopping, banking and information retrieval, various combinations of user hardware are required, depending upon the system used. To equip a home with the necessary hardware to provide two-way services can cost several thousand dollars today. A personal computer or a videotext decoder is required, and either way it's an expensive proposition. Whatever type of equipment is required, however, will have to drop in cost well below $500 to attract a large number of users. That figure is often considered a barrier for pricing strategy in consumer electronic products. But when consumer costs are considered, hardware costs are only part of the problem. In addition, a whole range of fees will have to be paid for installation, maintenance, subscriptions and transactions. The success of home services rides on the assumption that many households will be willing to pay between $25 and $100 a month for these services. In a society of diminished expectations, if they do come, they will largely be at the expense of other budget items.

Before making an investment in hardware and subscriber services, most people will have to be persuaded that what they are paying for will offer clear-cut advantages. Consumers are already asking themselves why they need an expensive home computer to balance a checkbook, or why they should subscribe to an electronic news service when they can get the news for "free" on television or for a few cents in the daily newspaper. One of the most effective ways to persuade people will be to offer them economic incentives to use the new media. The banking industry is doing this to some extent for customers who elect to carry out certain transactions using automated procedures. The banking industry's motivation stems as much from its determination to offset rising costs as it does from its desire to offer greater conveniences to its customers. Similarly, retailers and direct mail organizations could offer discounts on merchandise sold through electronic catalogs in order to encourage people to shop in this manner.

Electronic marketing relies on technology and many people fear technology. No matter how simple the systems are to operate, they are often perceived as "too complex." Many people are reminded of computers and computers are "too complicated" and "unfriendly." Personal computer manufacturers have created the image that working with their products is easy right from the beginning, but this is not really the case. Apple Computer Company has conceded that it takes an average of 20 hours for a neophyte to become proficient in using a personal computer. (When was the last time you spent 20 hours learning to operate a consumer product?) Manufacturers of personal computers have begun to recognize this problem, and they are now spending large sums of money to develop software that will make it easy and fast to master the intricacies of computer usage. Steps like this should help consumers overcome their fears.

A distinction can certainly be made between personal computers and an NEM technology such as videotext. The personal computer is powerful but somewhat difficult to use. Videotext is less powerful but relatively easy to use. In the minds of many consumers, however, all the new electronic media are lumped together and perceived as having something to do with computers. When technology is perceived as easy to use, consumers react positively. The phenomenal acceptance of video games is a case in point. Games are as easy to operate as the TV set itself. They are looked upon as fun, they give pleasure, and therefore they don't inspire the fear that technology often creates. Providers of new home services must persuade the public that their services are easy to use.

Early adoption of services supplied by the new electronic media, including electronic marketing, will become a rigorous exercise in market segmentation. The market must encompass the buying public, not only the computer professionals. It will actually be built on several segments, wherein groups of early adopter users can be identified and targeted. Examples of such segments include: professionals and small businessmen (many of whom work out of their homes), affluent consumers who can afford the cost of new technology and executives and white-collar workers from large organizations who will have the inclination or can be encouraged to do some of their work outside the office.

Students are another early adopter category which could become important, but for somewhat different reasons. Their exposure to computers in the academic environment will encourage them to stay close to and make use of technology at all times. The common thread pulling all this together will be the young, "computer literate" segment of the population weaned on television, proficient with video games and ready to make the fullest possible use of technology. As this group approaches or reaches its middle years by the end of this decade, and the mid-point of the next, it will provide a substantial market for many of the services that will undergo evaluation over the next five years or so.

It is from these groups that the first users of electronic banking, shopping and other services will emerge. Their use of such services will be secondary to business and professional use, which will be seen as justifying the initial cost of hardware and software. These groups will in no way constitute a mass market. The latter will develop over a longer period and on a highly selective basis. The mass market for home services using the new electronic media probably will never reach universal status like that of television or radio. In all likelihood, it won't exceed 40% of all households by the year 2000. Nevertheless, even 40% would be a tremendous number, since most estimates indicate that there will be about 100 million households by the end of the century. This should provide a large and active market for what will then be highly developed electronic services.

Support From the Business Community

In the competitive environment of the 1980s and 1990s, any organization, to survive, will have to improve its productivity and offer a high level of customer service. The full utilization of technology will be an imperative. In achieving these objectives a certain impetus will be provided for the support of electronic marketing.

Innovations in the banking and financial service industries are an example. These innovations all provide consumers benefits in terms of cost and convenience. However, the prime motivation to establish them came not from consumers but from businesses in their efforts to stay competitive, to enter new markets and to hold down costs. There is reason to believe that home banking and shopping will be supported by business for the very same reasons. They represent a natural progression of communication and data processing systems already developed. Over the long term, the consumer seems destined to be exposed to new services.

**Table 1.A: Major U.S. Videotext/Teletext Services
Suitable for Electronic Marketing**

Service (Owner)	Location	Start Date	Transmission Medium
CompuServe Information Service (H&R Block)	National (selected cities)	1979	Telephone
Indax (Cox Cable Communications)	San Diego, CA Omaha, NE	1982	Two-way Cable
Keyfax (Keycom Electronic Publishing)	National	1982	Satellite and Cable
Source Tele-computing Corp. (Reader's Digest Assn.)	National (selected cities)	1979	Telephone
Time Video Information Services (Time, Inc.)	San Diego, CA Orlando, FL	1982	Cable
Venture One (CBS/AT&T)	Ridgewood, NJ	Fall 1982	Telephone
Videotex America (Times Mirror Co./Infomart)	Mission Viejo, CA Palos Verdes, CA	March 1982	Two-way Cable Telephone
Viewtron (AT&T/Knight-Ridder Newspapers)	Coral Gables, FL South Florida	1980 July 1983	Telephone Telephone

**Table 1.A: Major U.S. Videotext/Teletext Services
Suitable for Electronic Marketing**

Number of Terminals	Status and Content
34,000	A two-way alphanumeric service* offering subscribers a wide range of data bases, including games, information and teleshopping through Comp-U-Store.
300 100	A trial service offering 7500 pages of news, information, banking (HomServ), shopping (Viewmart). Videotext channel to be supplemented with a shopping channel.
NA	A teletext service offering subscribers 100 pages of news, weather, sports, games and advertising. Initially broadcast on station WFLD (Chicago) on a trial basis.
25,000	A two-way alphanumeric service offering subscribers news, financial information, games, electronic mail and home banking.
400	A trial teletext service delivering 5000 pages of news, weather, sports, travel information, games and advertising from both local and national sources.
200	A trial videotext service offering 8000 pages of news, weather, sports, games, banking, shopping, messaging and advertising
150 200	A trial videotext service offering 70,000 pages of news, weather, sports, games, banking, shopping, messaging and advertising.
204	Initial trial in Coral Gables completed in 1981.
5,000	Commercial launch scheduled for mid-1983. A videotext service offering subscribers 70,000 pages of news, weather, sports, games, banking, shopping, messaging and advertising.

*Alphanumeric services consist almost exclusively of letters and numbers and occasionally include charts or primitive graphics.

Source: Knowledge Industry Publications, Inc. and the author.

2

Major Players in the Home Electronic Services Market

Many different types of organizations are likely to become catalysts for the home electronic services market. The infrastructure of such a market is already being created by a number of influential organizations engaged in communications, publishing, broadcasting and manufacturing, and some have begun to offer electronic marketing services on a limited scale.

Three major categories of participants figure to be involved in the process of shaping the home services market: system operators, service or information providers and hardware suppliers. American Telephone and Telegraph Company has the potential to fulfill all three roles, but most companies are far more limited in what they can offer. This chapter examines the different roles of these potential participants in home electronic services, with particular emphasis on their strengths and weaknesses with regard to electronic marketing.

SYSTEM OPERATORS

System operators are organizations that establish and maintain the telecommunications networks required to deliver home electronic services; they are likely to be companies who are already heavily involved in telecommunications, such as the telephone companies, cable TV companies, value-added networks (used for computer-to-computer data traffic), and TV broadcasters. Other types of broadcasters could become involved in system operations, such as AM and FM radio broadcasters, direct broadcast satellite operators, low power TV stations and multipoint distribution service operators.

System operators will be responsible for coordinating all the details necessary to provide functional service. These tasks will include technical and engineering support, communications, procurement of hardware and software, marketing, administration and customer service.

Several organizations specializing in telecommunications have already begun creating businesses as system operators. They include AT&T; General Telephone and Electronics Corp.; GTE Telenet Communications Corp.; CompuServe; Tymnet, Inc.; Cox Cable Communications; Dow Jones & Co., Inc.; CBS, Inc.; Time Inc. and The Times Mirror Company.

SERVICE AND INFORMATION PROVIDERS

The material that will flow back and forth giving the system its vitality will come from information and service providers. They can be called "infoserv" providers. Publishers, banks, retailers, direct marketers, financial service organizations, real estate firms, travel agents, sports and theatrical ticket brokers and legalized gambling services will all sign up as infoserv providers linked directly to user terminals in homes, offices and public locations. The new electronic media, by providing video presentation and interactive capability, will establish an unprecedented level of direct interaction between consumers and infoserv providers.

Infoserv providers will come mostly from businesses who are already serving the public, and they will use the new electronic media to reach new customers—or to provide better service to existing ones. In the early stages, use of the new media will complement the infoserv provider's established means of marketing: in-store selling, catalogs, direct mail, telephone and various types of advertising.

Although existing organizations who are well known to the public will enjoy a decided edge in serving consumers through electronic means, outsiders may also become important. Technology gives almost anyone the potential to reach consumers in the electronic marketplace. Realizing this potential will, of course, involve practical considerations that will effectively bar entry to many interested parties. Nevertheless, new participants can be expected.

An example of a new entrant relying on innovations in technology to serve the public is Comp-U-Store, a time-sharing service that offers an electronic catalog to personal computer users. Comp-U-Store provides customers access to a data base containing descriptions and prices for over 40,000 items covering a wide range of merchandise categories. (See Chapter 5 for a description of Comp-U-Store and its parent organization, Comp-U-Card of America.)

HARDWARE SUPPLIERS

Hardware suppliers will provide equipment to system operators, infoserv providers and system users. Equipment can be divided into two categories: industrial equipment, which is designed for running the system and which includes frame creation and storage terminals, special editing devices, character generators, headend computers and data processing facilities; and user equipment, which includes terminals, modems, decoders, keyboards, keypads and printers.

The industrial side of the market is already being supplied with a wide variety of equipment that can be used for electronic marketing. Led by Digital Equipment Corporation (DEC), computer makers have provided specialized software to allow their machines to perform many of the functions required in a videotext center. Norpak Ltd., a small Canadian firm, has also been a prominent supplier of such equipment. However, AT&T and IBM are now emerging as key suppliers. IBM has been selling hardware and software for videotext applications in Great Britain and West Germany. Most important, the trend of equipment suppliers since 1979 has been toward lower costs, which should encourage infoserv providers to begin assembling support systems for both business and home use.

The user side of the market is just beginning to see affordable hardware built to its specifications. Home computer makers, whose products did not initially appeal to mainstream home users, are now reconfiguring their products for the mass market. Apple Computer, Inc., Atari, Inc., Commodore Corporation, Radio Shack Corporation and Texas Instruments Inc. all figure prominently in the battle for the home computer market. TV manufacturers, at first reluctant to commit to the home services field, are now convinced that a market will exist. They are beginning to produce TV sets and add-ons that can convert an ordinary TV set into a computer terminal. Zenith Radio Corporation, RCA Corporation and Sony Corporation are ready to lead this movement.

Semiconductor manufacturers have long supported the efforts of other hardware makers by supplying chips. In the past, though, most of the chips were produced in small quantities, which made them expensive on a per-unit basis. With the creation of standard "chip sets" that are sold to several home equipment makers, the semiconductor manufacturers are able to lower their prices for components.

Hardware suppliers are gradually moving from skepticism to guarded optimism in terms of the consumer market for electronic services. By committing their design, production and marketing resources to a new market, the hardware suppliers will be able to deliver equipment at reasonable cost.

FUTURE LEADERS

Table 2.1 provides a capsule view of organizations who figure to play leading roles in the development of electronic marketing in the U.S. Admittedly, the list is somewhat arbitrary and could very well omit important organizations. However, the operative words for inclusion on the list are *leading roles*. These are the companies that will provide the leadership, the knowledge and the financial muscle over the next 10 years, the period during which home electronic services are expected to take root.

Comparison of different organizations within categories of expertise must be done carefully. For example, just because two companies are hardware suppliers does not necessarily mean that they will compete on an equal footing. AT&T will offer different capabilities than those of Tandy Corporation or Sony and it remains to be seen precisely which segments of the equipment market each will vie for.

Table 2.1 spells out the specific products and services that the leading organizations offer, and it should serve as a guide to the individual profiles that follow.

American Telephone & Telegraph Company

AT&T and its soon-to-be-divested operating companies could very well dominate the emerging home services market, although the newspaper, cable and data processing industries will fight vigorously to prevent this. Despite government and industry attempts to create more competition, AT&T and its subsidiaries continue to dominate both long-distance and local communications service, although the giant utility's share of the market is slowly declining. Nevertheless, it is hard to see what will prevent AT&T and the newly independent operating companies from market domination.

AT&T took a big step forward when it introduced its videotext frame terminal at the Videotex '82 Conference held in New York City. This piece of equipment, offered at $34,000, can be used for frame creation, editing, formatting and interframe linking. Viewdata Corporation of America, Inc. was the first customer, placing an order for 25 units for delivery beginning in August 1982. CBS, Inc. is using this device for its videotext trial in Ridgewood, NJ.

AT&T and the independent telephone companies start out with a number of important advantages: telephone service is universal, reaching virtually every home and office in the nation; the switching capability of the system can connect any two phones or terminals throughout the world instantaneously; manufacturing and distribution capability for a wide range of

Table 2.1: Future Leaders in Home Electronic Services, 1983-1993

Company	System Operator	Information/Service (Infoserv) Provider	Hardware Supplier	Products and/or Services
American Express Company		X		Financial and travel services
AT&T (American Bell)	X	X	X	Communications networks, terminals, Yellow Pages directories
Cox Cable	X			Cable TV, consumer data base services
CBS, Inc.	X	X		Broadcasting, publishing, videotext, teletext
Dow Jones & Company		X		Publishing, data base services
IBM			X	Personal computers, software
Knight-Ridder Newspapers	X	X		Publishing, videotext
Sears, Roebuck & Company		X	X	Retailing, financial services, hardware
Sony Corporation			X	Terminals, decoders, personal computers
Tandy Corporation (Radio Shack)			X	Terminals, decoders, personal computer
Time Inc.	X	X		Cable TV, teletext, publishing
The Times Mirror Company	X	X		Cable TV, videotext, publishing

Source: Knowledge Industry Publications, Inc., and the author.

telecommunications equipment is very strong; and a substantial published data base is already in place in the form of directories and Yellow Pages.

AT&T, the independents and the Bell operating companies, either individually or collectively, are in a position to play the roles of network operator, service and information provider and hardware supplier. The first and last roles appear reasonably certain; the crucial issue is what the industry will be allowed to do as a service and information provider. By putting its Yellow Pages directories online, the telephone industry could become a leading electronic publisher, with severe repercussions for the newspaper industry; and by offering its data processing services to customers, it may come to dominate certain areas of that industry as well. The role that AT&T will be allowed to play is one of the most significant public policy issues of the day and will have to be clarified through legislative and judicial efforts. The manner in which this is resolved will be crucial to the direction of the home electronic services market.

International Business Machines Corporation

"Big Blue," as some people refer to IBM, is moving quietly to secure a dominant position in the electronic services market. Its activities in Europe offer some clues to its future strategy. It is already providing service bureau facilities in England; it has developed software packages for Prestel and Bildschirmtext, the national videotext systems in England and West Germany, respectively; and it is offering private videotext services for business users in England based on its Series/1 computer.

By the end of 1982, IBM was offering the Series/1 videotext system to U.S. business users, who can set up an installation for as little as $60,000. Private videotext systems can be used internally by many organizations for electronic mail, operational data, travel information and as a company-wide bulletin board. IBM's personal computer, which was introduced in August 1981, could be attractive to the upper end of the home market.

IBM's initial strategy is obviously geared to serving the business market. Over the longer term, it may not enter the home market directly. However, it is conceivable that it may serve as a systems operator relying on outside partners such as banks, publishers or retailers to handle direct contact with the public. The communications network to reach individual households could be furnished by cable operators or the divested Bell operating companies.

Sears, Roebuck & Co.

Retailing made Sears what it is today. Nevertheless, its retail operations have run into rough weather over the past few years. The company has changed course several times, employing various merchandising strategies in an attempt to find a strategy that would ensure steady growth and stability. In the meantime other mass merchandisers, notably K Mart Corporation and J.C. Penney Co., Inc., have increased their market share at Sears' expense. Sears' merchandise group accounted for $20.2 billion in 1981, or 74% of total revenue. However, merchandising contributed only 43% to pretax income.

Sears recognized some time ago that its type of retailing no longer offers the growth possibilities that existed from the end of World War II until the mid-1970s. Economic stagnation, inflation and social and demographic changes, along with increased competition, are all responsible for major changes in retailing. Discounters, at one end, and high-priced specialty operations, at the other, have fared much better than retailers like Sears who have concentrated on a middle-of-the-road merchandising approach.

Consequently, Sears has embarked on an ambitious diversification strategy that will de-emphasize retail operations. Sears has identified the financial services as a high-growth field, and it is taking aggressive steps to enter that market. Sears has long had a nucleus of financial service organizations, including Allstate Insurance Co. and Allstate Savings and Loan Association. To this group it has recently added Dean Witter Reynolds Organization Inc., a leading stock brokerage concern, and Coldwell Banker & Co., one of the nation's largest real estate brokerage firms. Sears' chairman, Edward L. Telling, has announced Sears' intention of "becoming one of the largest financial service companies in the United States."[1]

Bold as these steps may be, they in no way suggest that Sears is about to abandon the retail business that has been its mainstay for so many years. Sears is examining the application of new technologies for retailing. It has participated in several videotext trials, including the much publicized Viewtron test conducted by Knight-Ridder Newspapers, Inc. and AT&T in Coral Gables, FL, during 1980 and 1981 (see Chapter 5). In addition Sears has run a test using optical video disc technology for one of its catalogs.

These steps suggest that Sears could become one of the first retailers and direct-mail organizations to offer a "teleshopping" package to its customers via videotext, video disc or possibly a combination of both. Furthermore, financial services, such as real estate, mortgages, insurance and securities brokerage could be included to enhance the value of such a package, and such services might be accessible by using the Sears charge card.

Sears will probably restrict its role to infoserv provider rather than system operator. It could also be a supplier of low-cost user hardware for

---

[1]Sears, Roebuck & Company, *Annual Report*, 1981.

videotext and teletext, such as computer terminals, decoders and printers. Sears has been a supplier of decoder devices for closed captioning services used by hearing-impaired viewers. It turned down an opportunity to form a joint venture with COMSAT which has received FCC approval for a direct-to-home broadcast satellite (DBS) service. Sears' function would have been the sales, installation and servicing of the antennas and decoders required for in-home satellite broadcasting reception. No one else has joined COMSAT.

Rumors have circulated from time to time regarding a possible linkup between Sears and IBM. Under such an arrangement IBM would manufacture a low-cost videotext terminal that Sears would distribute to consumers. Such a venture seems unlikely for the foreseeable future.

Radio Shack Corporation

Radio Shack, the retail arm of Tandy Corporation, has worked its way to the top of the competitive consumer electronics field. Sales are expected to exceed $2 billion by fiscal 1983. With over 8100 outlets worldwide, it specializes in private label merchandise, much of which it manufactures. It has succeeded largely by developing a distinctive image in the consumer's mind for a wide variety of end products and system components. A judicious selection of product line offerings has kept it out of such highly discounted items as TVs and video cassette recorders (VCRs). On the other hand, it did take a successful plunge into low-priced personal computers. Its TRS-80 series was the top-selling line until challenged first by Apple and now by IBM.

Radio Shack was one of the first retailers to recognize that personal computers would not sell in large numbers unless supported by economical and easy-to-use software. As a result, it now offers a wide variety of software that can be used with its TRS-80 line. It has gone a step further by offering software and specific applications such as CompuServe, a time-sharing information utility that offers information and transactional services to subscribers through a personal computer.

Radio Shack has a number of things going for it as an important participant in the emerging home services market. Its strengths include universal consumer recognition, strong distribution capability, moderate technological prowess and substantial control over manufacturing. Its biggest shortcoming is its lack of communications capability, but this could be overcome through joint venture arrangements with partners specializing in telecommunications.

Sony Corporation

Sony is often acknowledged to be the premier manufacturing company in the highly competitive consumer electronics field. It has an obvious role to play as a key supplier of hardware for home electronics systems. The company is already a market leader in the production of TV sets, VCRs and video cameras for the home market. It is also a key supplier of a wide variety of TV equipment for the broadcast and industrial video markets. In Europe, it is supplying videotext terminals that can be used with Prestel. Sony is in partnership with ABC Video Enterprises, Inc. to develop the Home View Network, a program service that ABC stations will transmit to subscriber VCRs for playback. Sony decoders will be provided to process the signal, which will be transmitted in scrambled form.

MEDIA ORGANIZATIONS

Many different types of organizations serve the public with newspapers, magazines and broadcasting services. These organizations perceive electronic marketing and electronic publishing activities both as a threat and as an opportunity to enhance existing services. Newspapers are concerned about the impact of electronic publishing on major revenue producers such as classified and display advertising and special supplements. Magazines, many of which have evolved into special-interest vehicles, are also closely watching the new media. They are particularly interested in the course that cable takes, since it is developing its own special-interest programming strategy through a profusion of narrowcast networks.

The position of broadcasting in all of this is equally uncertain. The new media have failed to drain off significant advertising revenues as yet. However, over the long run, they will inevitably attract increasing amounts of advertising dollars. The networks and local TV stations should continue to attract the greatest proportion of advertising revenues, but they will become less efficient in reaching large numbers of consumers with their commercial messages as sponsors begin to shift a larger proportion of their advertising budget into alternative media.

Five media companies will play major roles in the emerging electronic marketing environment: Knight-Ridder Newspapers, Dow Jones & Company, The Times-Mirror Company, Time Inc. and CBS, Inc. All are expected to become important information and service providers, and in some cases, system operators. All of these companies are actively engaged in testing videotext, teletext or both.

Knight-Ridder Newspapers

Knight-Ridder derived 92% of its $1.2 billion in 1981 revenues from its newspaper interests, which include *The Miami Herald* and *The Philadelphia Inquirer*. Viewdata Corporation of America, a subsidiary of Knight-Ridder, and AT&T have formed a joint venture which has offered an experimental videotext system, Viewtron. During 1980 and 1981, the system was tested in 160 Coral Gables, FL, homes. The test, which cost some $2 million, ended in September 1981. (Details are discussed in Chapter 5.) An expanded test planned for 5000 South Florida homes is scheduled for 1983. Knight-Ridder has announced that it will form joint ventures with other newspaper publishers to offer videotext service in local markets. Partners already announced for such an arrangement include Capital Cities Communications, Inc., publisher of *The Kansas City Star/Times* and *The Fort Worth Star-Telegram,* and Affiliated Publications, Inc., publisher of *The Boston Globe*.

Dow Jones & Company

Dow Jones relies heavily on print media for most of its revenues. Of its $641 million 1981 revenues, newspapers and magazines accounted for 86%. Its lead publications are *The Wall Street Journal* and *Barron's*. Dow Jones and Knight-Ridder failed in their bid for a joint takeover of UA-Columbia Cablevision Inc. when they were nosed out by Rogers Cablesystems and United Artists Theatre Circuit, Inc. in 1981. However, Dow Jones does own a 25% interest in Continental Cablevision, a multiple system operator with some 500,000 basic subscribers, and, through a joint venture with Prime Cable Company, it holds the franchise for the Princeton, NJ, cable system which, when completed, is designed to be a showcase for many interactive services. Dow Jones has already tested the distribution of information to the home market via cable TV. These tests were conducted in Danbury, CT, through its Ottaway Newspapers Inc. subsidiary, and in Dallas, TX, through Sammons Communications, Inc., a large multiple system operator. The Dow Jones/News Retrieval Service is available to users of personal computers. This service is discussed in Chapter 5.

The Times Mirror Company

Times Mirror is a media conglomerate with interests in publishing, broadcasting and cable. Its newspaper operations accounted for 51% of 1981 revenues, which reached $2.16 billion. It has been actively involved in testing videotext and cable shopping services. In early 1982 Times Mirror Videotex Services, Inc. started a videotext test in 350 Southern California homes offering both information retrieval and transactional services. This test ran through the end of 1982. A larger trial has been hinted at for 1983 dependent upon results with the first 350 homes. The trial service offered some 70,000 pages, including news and retail and classified advertising from *The Los Angeles Times,* and travel information and home banking through the Bank of America. Times Mirror Videotex Services, Inc. has formed a joint venture with Infomart, owned by Canadian publishers Southam and Torstar (*Toronto Star*). This joint undertaking, known as Videotex America, will promote turnkey videotext systems to operators throughout the U.S.

In an earlier venture, Times Mirror Cable tested a cable shopping service in conjunction with Comp-U-Card of America. However, this venture never went beyond the trial stage, and Comp-U-Card plans to develop the service in cooperation with Metromedia. (See Chapter 5 for discussion of the Times Mirror videotext trial.)

Time Inc.

Time Inc. is another media giant with major interests in publishing and cable television. 1981 revenues reached $3.3 billion with 26% from magazines and 19% from a rapidly growing video operation. Its print publications include *Time, People, Fortune, Money* and *Sports Illustrated.* Its cable subsidiary, American Television Communications (ATC), with over 2 million basic subscribers by the end of 1982, was running neck and neck with Tele-Communications, Inc. for the top spot among multiple system operators (MSOs).

Time's pay cable network, Home Box Office (HBO) dominates the field, reaching 11 million subscribers, or nearly 80% of the pay cable market. In 1981, Time purchased a one-third interest in USA Network, a basic cable network. Time is developing a teletext system that will be distributed by satellite to cable systems. It will draw heavily on its own editorial resources, and it will also use national and local services from outside sources.

CBS, Inc.

Total revenues for CBS in 1981 reached $4.13 billion with media activities accounting for 76%. CBS is moving on several important fronts in the new electronic media. Unfortunately, its most publicized venture was ill fated. CBS Cable, a basic cable network that specialized in programming for the performing arts, announced that it would discontinue operations by the end of 1982. In 1982 CBS formed a joint venture with Twentieth Century-Fox Film Corporation to produce software for the home video and cable markets.

Under an FCC waiver, CBS is permitted to acquire cable systems with a consolidated total of 90,000 subscribers. It plans to use any systems that it acquires for testing new hardware and software. So far it has acquired only one system, Black Hawk Cable Communication Company, located in Fort Worth, TX, with 17,000 subscribers.

CBS is involved in planning for or testing several new technologies including teletext, videotext and high definition television (HDTV).

Its teletext system, known as Extravision, has been tested on KNXT, the CBS-owned station in Los Angeles. It could become one of the first organizations to go national with teletext by offering the service through CBS television affiliates.

CBS has a major interest in testing electronic publishing. Its own publishing resources include specialty magazines such as *Road and Track, Mechanix Illustrated, Woman's Day* and *Field and Stream*. These publications will be an important part of a videotext test which was launched in late 1982 by CBS and AT&T in 200 Ridgewood, NJ, homes, designated as "Venture One," which will incorporate home banking, shopping and information retrieval.

AT&T will provide communications and software support, using some of the systems that it had planned to use in Austin, TX, for an electronic Yellow Pages trial that was cancelled due to opposition from the newspaper industry. Automatic Data Processing (ADP), a data processing company, will also be involved, providing support for a bank-at-home capability that will be included in Venture One.

CBS' commitment to videotext is difficult to judge at this time. Clearly it wants to establish a position of leadership, and it is well ahead of NBC and also ABC in most areas. However, the content of the Venture One data base will be drawn largely from existing CBS publications. Unlike Time Inc., which is prepared to spend what is necessary to develop an "original look," CBS is being conservative and relying on recycled material. Venture One could be a more productive trial for AT&T and ADP to test systems, hardware, software and communications than it will be for CBS.

Cox Cable Communications

Cox Cable, a subsidiary of Cox Broadcasting, is the fourth largest MSO, having slightly more than 1 million basic subscribers at the end of

1981. It operates the nation's largest single system, in San Diego, with 211,000 basic subscribers, and its newest franchises in Omaha and New Orleans became operational in 1982.

Cox has always placed emphasis on the development and use of state-of-the-art engineering and equipment. Cox's version of videotext is an interactive service called Index (Interactive Data Exchange) which it began testing in early 1982 in 200 San Diego homes. Cox is reported to have spent more than $10 million (some estimates run much higher) in developing Index, which provides home banking, shopping and information retrieval capability. (See Chapter 5 for details on Index.) Cox has had to endure repeated delays in the delivery of Index home terminals from Oak Communications, a major supplier to the cable industry. The company has also encountered more than its share of the engineering and software development problems that can normally be expected when state-of-the-art systems are developed.

Cox's strategy to develop non-entertainment services is unique in the cable industry. There is considerable skepticism within the industry about the eventual level of consumer demand for such services. Most cable operators have been content to rely on entertainment, which has provided a steadily increasing stream of revenues from basic and pay service.

Furthermore, there is the sobering realization that AT&T and its soon-to-be-divested operating companies could compete with cable for the home services market. Such a possibility looms even larger if the local operating companies make a massive investment in fiber optic technology, which would give them broadband capability (the capability to carry a large volume of information) comparable to that of the newest cable systems. Nevertheless, to win new franchises and to retain old ones, practically every cable proposal written today includes two-way capability. For this reason Cox is expected to stick with its Index program, even though profitable operations cannot be expected for many years. One way that Cox could recoup its investment is through licensing Index to other cable operators. However, little interest can be expected from cable before Index proves to be a reliable and profitable system.

American Express Company

Although the financial and travel service industries are highly fragmented, American Express is a dominant company in both, with significant potential to be heavily involved in electronic marketing. American Express' primary consumer businesses are credit card operations, travelers checks, travel services and direct marketing. Each of these services will find growing applications in electronic marketing. The same is true for some of the financial services offered by Shearson Loeb Rhoades, Inc., the securities brokerage concern it acquired in 1981.

American Express entered the cable field in 1979 when it purchased a 50% interest in Warner Cable, resulting in a name change to Warner Amex Cable Communications Inc. This company has been successfully bidding for new franchises, and during the 1980-1981 period, it was awarded franchises in Cincinnati, Houston, Pittsburgh, Dallas and suburban St. Louis. It has since been awarded the franchise in Milwaukee, and it could conceivably win three additional franchises in the unwired boroughs of New York City.

Warner Amex Cable has attracted a great deal of attention due to Qube, an interactive system which was initially installed in Columbus, OH, and which is now scheduled to be included in every major Warner Amex Cable franchise. The investment in Qube is estimated to have exceeded $25 million. The initial Qube system was not designed for transactional use but upgraded versions will be, although Warner Amex's long-term commitment to transactional services has yet to be convincingly demonstrated. Some of its Qube subscribers in Columbus, equipped with Atari personal computers, are testing transactional services.

American Express has used videotext extensively in Europe for electronic marketing. The British Prestel system and the French Teletel system have both carried pages supplied by American Express, which viewers can call up on their screens to make travel arrangements and to order merchandise from a video catalog.

OTHER INFLUENTIAL INDUSTRIES

Other organizations will have an important influence on the development of electronic marketing. They include retailers, direct marketers, equipment suppliers and financial service organizations.

As a group, retail organizations have not been leaders in developing electronic marketing. They will probably not join in until others have blazed a trail. Three organizations worth watching are: Federated Department Stores, Inc. (which holds an investment in Comp-U-Card of America); Dayton-Hudson Corporation (a participant in the Viewtron trial through its subsidiary, B. Dalton Co.); and Fingerhut Corporation, a direct marketing subsidiary of American Can Company (Fingerhut's subsidiaries are Viewmart, Inc. and HomServ, Inc., both involved in the development of transactional services for Index—see Chapter 5).

Equipment suppliers who could eventually play key roles include Apple,

Atari, RCA Corporation, Zenith Radio Corporation, Motorola, Inc., Mattel, Inc., Oak Industries Inc., Matsushita Electric Industrial Company, Ltd., Pioneer Electronic Corporation, Toshiba Corporation and Matra S.A. Despite the importance of every one of these firms, their eventual roles are not yet well defined.

The financial services industry, led by commercial banks, has been the most active in developing hardware, software and support systems for electronic marketing. Through 1982, the cumulative investment in almost two dozen trials offering home banking could reach $150 million, with most of this having come since mid-1981.

The banks at the leading edge of this movement include Citibank, N.A., Chase Manhattan Bank, N.A., Chemical Bank, Bank of America National Trust and Savings Assn. and Financial Interstate Services, Inc. (formerly United American Service Corp.). Motivated largely by rising costs and competitive factors, the banks are actively investigating new methods to deliver services to their customers. This search has spurred the development of automatic teller machines (ATMs) and telephone bill payment systems (TBPs), and it is now leading to the development of home banking systems based on videotext.

Initially, videotext bank services may have greater success with small businesses than with individuals. To be successful with consumers, banks will have to provide diversified services, including electronic marketing, publishing and mail. However, the banking package may be offered first, since it could be used on a regular basis to perform routine functions quickly and economically.

Unlike other banks conducting home banking tests, First Bank System, Inc. (FBS) of Minneapolis is not nationally known. However, FBS does have the distinction of operating the first electronic network that was a complete system, FirstHand. Agricultural information, such as farm commodity prices, was the most important part of the service. In addition, banking, shopping and information retrieval services were offered. (*The Minneapolis Star & Tribune* had originally planned to participate but later withdrew its support.) Users were supplied with a compact terminal equipped with a nine-inch black and white screen, a modem for the telephone connection and an alphanumeric keyboard.

By appealing to agribusiness users, FBS carefully segmented its market. It identified users in isolated, rural communities who would find it very convenient to bank and shop from home and who had a continuous need for information, much of it related to agricultural transactions. By offering a basket of services FBS gave FirstHand wider appeal than it would have had as a banking service alone.

MAKING THE PIECES FIT

The companies discussed in this chapter clearly have the pieces to fit into the complicated mosaic of electronic services that can be delivered by the new media. However, the extent of their involvement and the rate at which plans are put into practice will vary widely depending upon management's sense of urgency and interpretation of the future.

Just having the pieces in no way ensures eventual success. The intricate coordination of many different elements will be required. New strategies and operational procedures will have to be developed. In most cases, many of the elements will be beyond the effective control or capability of any individual participant, thus necessitating joint venture efforts. An organization may be tempted to leap far beyond areas of strength and expertise to achieve certain goals. The trick will be to take entrepreneurial steps but in a prudent way—something that is easier said than done.

The key to success is cooperative relationships, which will bring together complementary resources from within an organization or from the outside. The entertainment field has already moved quite far in bringing together different types of organizations to deliver services for cable TV and home video. The movement has just started in the non-entertainment area. The creation of symbiotic relationships from such mergers will put management to the severest of tests.

3

Direct Marketing in the Electronic Age

The shopping malls of the future will still be out on the American highways, but millions of shoppers will not visit them. Sophisticated communications equipment will be located in homes, offices and public places, making possible widespread electronic shopping for many goods and services.

Selling without stores is nothing new. It is known as *direct marketing,* and it has been gaining in popularity over the past decade.

DIRECT MARKETING DEFINED

Because direct marketing has been affected by changes brought about by technological, social and economic forces, its definition has been changing. The Direct Marketing Association (DMA) has recognized this. Currently, DMA defines direct marketing as "an interactive system of marketing which uses one or more advertising media to effect a measurable response and/or transaction at any location." Interestingly, this is the first time that the term *interactive* has crept into the definition, although it is used often to describe one of the salient features of the new electronic media.

Direct marketing is often thought of as just direct mail, but it includes much more. In addition to mail, it can use radio, TV, telephone, print ads and coupons, store catalogs, package inserts, bill stuffers and even matchbook covers.

Compared to "regular" newspaper, magazine, radio and TV advertising direct marketing is *interactive* since it is designed to elicit a response to a specific offer. Electronic marketing (which can also be termed "teleservices marketing") is a notch above "conventional" forms of direct marketing since not only can the consumer establish communications instantaneously with an advertiser, merchant or service provider but he can do this *visually* and he can *control* the sequence and content of the dialog. Furthermore, this can be done on a 24-hour-a-day basis from practically any location in the world provided the right type of equipment and communications system is available. It creates a very different experience (interaction) from traditional shopping or direct marketing methods. When using the latter, the closest thing to teleservice marketing is talking by telephone to a teleservices clerk, not quite the same thing as an interactive, visual exchange which can be controlled by the customer. (See Table 3.1).

THE DEVELOPMENT OF DIRECT MARKETING

Direct marketing started out in the nineteenth century as direct mail used by retailers.[1] Montgomery Ward published the first mail-order catalog in 1872, and was followed by Richard Sears in 1886. The U.S. postal system, aided by the development of a national railway system, was to boost catalog shopping since it gave retailers a cost-effective means of shipping merchandise to customers who lived beyond traditional local service areas and who were often located in remote areas of the country. The initial mail order catalogs of the late nineteenth century developed as a generalized response to the socioeconomic needs of a changing society. Mail-order merchandising for specific market segments developed much later; today, Sears, Roebuck & Co. issues over three dozen different catalogs to cover every conceivable segment of the mail-order market.

Two significant developments in the direct mail business took place in the 1920s. First, national publications such as *Time, The New Yorker* and *The Saturday Review Of Literature* came on the scene. These magazines created an environment for direct mail literature supplied by organizations such as the Book-of-the-Month Club, founded in 1926. Second, a special bulk mail rate (third class) was established in 1928 by the U.S. Postal Service. This classification made it possible for large-scale direct mail offerings on a cost-effective basis.

Direct Mail

The mass merchandise direct mail operations of Sears, J.C. Penney Co., Inc., Montgomery Ward & Co., Inc. and others dominated the field from the late nineteenth century until World War II. The post-World-War-II period, marked by growing consumer affluence in contrast to the depression period of the 1930s, saw the development of numerous specialty mail-order operations such as Spencer Gifts, Sunset House, Foster and

---

[1]Much of the following information comes from the 1981 and 1982 *Fact Books on Direct Response Marketing* (New York: Direct Marketing Association).

Table 3.1:   Comparison of Marketing Methods

Method	Consumer Response Capability	Time Required to Establish Interaction	Geographic Restrictions	Variety of Products & Services	Technological Support Required
Retailing	Limited hours	Extensive	Local only	Unlimited	None
Direct Marketing	Mixed	Mixed	None	Limited	Limited
Teleservices (Electronic) Marketing	Unlimited	None	None	Limited	Extensive

Source: Compiled by the author.

Gallagher, Inc., Hanover House Industries, Inc. and Fingerhut Corporation. It was during this period that Time-Life Books and the Columbia Record and Tape Club came into existence. The trend toward specialization has continued over the past ten years. Two of the best examples are the Horchow Collection, with its wide variety of fine housewares, and the mail-order house, JS&A, which offers a bewildering array of the latest in consumer electronics gadgetry, many offered to the public for the first time.

In some cases, obscure retailers have catapulted to national prominence through direct marketing. L.L. Bean is an example. This company has operated with a single store in Freeport, ME, since 1912, specializing in rugged outerwear and camping goods. Until the mid-1970s, it was almost unknown outside the immediate area that it served. However, by establishing a mail-order program, L.L. Bean developed a national following. In 1982 its direct sales are expected to reach $150 million, and it will distribute 35 million copies of its catalogs to consumers in every part of the nation. Table 3.2 provides a list of leading direct marketers during 1981 and their estimated sales.

If used effectively, direct mail is a powerful tool in reaching target markets. According to Bob Stone, chairman of the board of Stone & Adler, Inc., one of the largest advertising agencies specializing in direct marketing by using direct mail: "You can select a mailing list that zeroes in on a certain type of person or a specific geographic area. You can pick people with a known interest or a specific buying history, with little or no waste circulation. And you can make your message a personal one by using a computer letter that addresses each individual by name or you can use a printed letter that includes copy directed to the specific lists selected."[2]

Telephone Marketing

Wide Area Telephone Service (WATS) lines have increased the value of the telephone to direct marketers. With the sharply increased cost of personal (as opposed to telephone) sales calls, the telephone has become a highly favored sales tool.

With segmented lists made available through data processing procedures, the telephone can be used to service prospective customers on both an incoming and outgoing basis with pinpoint accuracy. The telephone can be used in conjunction with other promotional techniques such as TV and print commercials and direct mail, or it can be used independently. The message can be conveyed by a "live communicator" or it can be partially or even fully taped. However, using the telephone for direct contact be-

---

[2]Bob Stone, *Successful Direct Marketing Methods* (Chicago: Crain Books, 1979).

Table 3.2: Sales Volume of Leading Direct Marketers, 1981
(in millions)

Company	Sales volume
Sears, Roebuck & Co.	$1,646
J.C. Penney Co.	1,537
Montgomery Ward & Co. (Mobil)	1,231
Time Life Books	400
Spiegel (Otto Versand)	387
Franklin Mint Corp.	375
Fingerhut Corp. (American Can Co.)	300
Aldens (Wickes Corp.)	260
Signature Financial Marketing (Wards)	200
Columbia Record Club	195
Publishers Clearing House	170
American Express Co.	140
Grolier	135
L.L. Bean	132
Heath Co. (Zenith Corp.)	115
Avon Fashions	100
Hanover House Industries	100
Herrschner, Brookstone & Joseph Bank (Quaker Oats)	100
RCA	100
Spencer Gifts (MCA)	85
Current Inc. (Looart)	70
Dreyfus Corp.	60
Book-of-the-Month Club (Time Inc.)	60
Swiss Colony	53
Roaman's	50
Eddie Bauer (General Mills)	43
Horchow	40
Lillian Vernon Corp.	40
Miles Kimball	40
Figi's (American Can Co.)	35
Harry & David	35
Lee Wards (General Mills)	35

Note: Estimated figures. Revenues of some organizations are less than figures reported independently due to adjustments made by DMA based on a redefinition of what constitutes direct marketing sales.

Source: *1982 Fact Book on Direct Response Marketing* (New York: Direct Marketing Association, Inc.), p. 80. Reprinted with permission.

tween customers and suppliers is a less sophisticated approach to electronic marketing since the benefit of online, visual display made possible by direct consumer interaction with a computerized data base is missing.

Newspaper Preprints

As illustrated in Table 3.3, newspaper preprints are the third largest category of direct marketing advertising expenditures. Preprints can be free-standing inserts in a regular newspaper or they can be distributed via one of the syndicated Sunday supplements. In some cases direct response ads are run like conventional newspaper ads (referred to as run of press or ROP). However, these ads do not have the impact of a preprinted ad run as an insert or a special supplement.

Table 3.3: Total Direct Marketing Advertising Expenditures: 1980 vs. 1981 (in millions)

Categories	1980	1981
Telephone	$ 9,845.0	$11,476.0
Direct Mail	9,998.7	10,566.7
Newspaper Preprints	2,032.4	2,228.5
Television	253.0	295.0
Consumer Magazines	135.0	150.0
Newspapers	73.0	60.6
Business Magazines	53.0	59.0
Radio	26.0	29.0
Totals	$22,487.9	$25,031.8

Source: *1982 Fact Book on Direct Response Marketing* (New York: Direct Marketing Association, Inc.), p. 1. Reprinted with permission.

Direct Marketing Advertising Expenditures

Total direct marketing advertising expenditures as reported by the DMA are estimated to have reached almost $22.5 billion in 1980 and over $25 billion in 1981. They are broken down in Table 3.3. Note that direct mail and telephone methods account for nearly 90% of all direct marketing advertising expenditures.

THE GROWTH OF DIRECT MARKETING

Based on figures released by the DMA, direct marketing sales topped $120 billion in 1981, up from $112 billion in 1980. Direct marketing has grown almost three times faster than conventional retailing over the past few years. The total direct marketing figure includes consumer and industrial sales and money raised for not-for-profit activities. Of the total, consumer direct marketing sales ran between $40 and $45 billion in 1981, up from $36 billion in 1980, according to the DMA. Maxwell Sroge, a direct marketing consulting firm, has reported that the leading sales categories in 1980 were: ready-to-wear clothing, $5.1 billion; books, $1.4 billion; sporting goods, $780 million; and food, $500 million. Of even greater significance, pretax profits of direct mail, an important part of direct marketing, have been estimated at 10%, compared to 6% for in-store selling, according to a survey conducted by the National Retail Merchants' Association.

The significance of direct marketing is that it gives almost any organization, whether directly serving the public or not, the ability to reach consumers, businesses, donors and the like without having to depend upon physical locations.

Indications are that direct marketing has not hurt retailing. A great deal of direct marketing is carried on by retailers themselves as an extension of their business. Many of the direct marketers who are not involved in retailing are specialty operations offering merchandise that is unavailable or hard to find in retail stores.

Teleshopping, or electronic marketing, will help direct marketing by providing another powerful tool to get the job done. Teleshopping could have a real impact on retailing over the long term. This impact could be felt in a wide range of retail categories. However, it is anticipated that retailers will adopt teleshopping for their own use rather than allowing competitors to take it over. They will do this in the same way that they have harnessed direct marketing for their own use.

Ogilvy & Mather International conducted a telephone study of 1500 respondents in November 1978. The objective of the study was to determine consumer attitudes and behavior in regard to direct response. The study reveals two very interesting findings. First, 65% of the respondents had conducted a direct marketing transaction within the past 12 months. Second, 23% had spent $100 or more on direct marketing transaction(s), and this group accounted for 83% of the total dollar volume. The study also reveals the percentage of respondents who had made purchases in specific categories (see Table 3.4).

Table 3.4:   Direct Marketing Transactions by Major Categories, 1978

Category of Purchases	Percent of Respondents*
Magazines	54
Books, book club memberships	33
Shoes, clothing	27
Records, tapes, cassettes	23
Credit cards	22
Seeds, plants, garden supplies	20

*Total exceeds 100% because respondents indicated multiple responses.

Source: *1982 Fact Book on Direct Response Marketing* (New York: Direct Marketing Association, Inc.) p. 17. Reprinted by permission.

Products with fewest purchases included insurance, home-study programs, home furnishings and hi-fi stereo equipment. Note that figures reveal percentages of respondents who made transactions—they do not show the dollar value of each category. A low-percentage category could conceivably have a high dollar value, and the opposite is also true.

DIRECT MARKETING VS. MASS MARKETING

Direct marketing has grown rapidly over the past few years for many reasons:

- Energy costs have made transportation to stores expensive.

- Rising crime rates have restricted the movement of many people, especially in urban areas.

- More women than ever before are working and must budget their shopping time.

- People moving to new communities wish to retain existing relationships with merchants and service providers.

- The level of service at many retail stores has declined.

- Direct marketers can specialize more than most retailers can.

Some less obvious factors are important too. A multitude of new values, attitudes and lifestyles are emerging to challenge the mass conformity of earlier times. The "me" generation of the 1960s has reached adulthood and it is demanding a wider variety of products and services than earlier generations did.

The job of the media planner has become increasingly complex due to fundamental changes in the media structure itself. Broadcast TV, which once monopolized the viewer's attention, must now compete with the distractions created by cable, pay TV, VCRs, video disc players, video games and personal computers. The mass audiences that advertisers have relied on broadcast TV to deliver for the past 30 years are being steadily eroded by all the diversionary options that are becoming available. New methods must be devised if advertisers hope to reach the steadily growing number of viewers who are spending less time watching broadcast television.

While their parent organizations have concentrated their creative powers on a relatively small array of print and broadcast media, the direct marketing arms of the agencies have been more adventurous, experimenting with a variety of direct mail catalogs and other media. It is from these organizations that Madison Avenue's early support for the new electronic media—especially cable TV—is emerging.

Marketers have responded by offering a growing variety of products. To position these products, direct marketing can often be used effectively to supplement traditional marketing methods. It can be particularly effective if specific markets and high probability prospects have been identified. This is the rifle rather than the shotgun approach to marketing.

Role of the Advertising Industry in Direct Marketing

The high growth rate achieved by direct marketing has attracted the attention of Madison Avenue. Many agencies have organized direct marketing departments or have taken over existing firms. Young and Rubicam International, Inc., ranked number one in 1981 in world billings and income, owns three direct response agencies: Stone & Adler, Wunderman Ricotta & Kline, Inc. and Chapman Direct Marketing, Inc. Rapp and Collins is a part of Doyle Dane Bernbach, Inc., and Schwab-Beatty is owned by Marsteller, Inc. Other direct marketing firms which are part of large agencies include Ogilvy & Mather Direct Response Inc., Ayer Direct, Grey Direct Marketing Group, Soskin-Thompson (J. Walter Thompson Co.) and Compton Direct Marketing. (See Table 3.5 for a list of the leading direct marketing firms and their estimated billings in 1980 and 1981.)

TECHNOLOGICAL DEVELOPMENTS IN DIRECT MARKETING

Advances in technology, telecommunications and credit authorization procedures have been key factors in the growth of direct marketing. Fur-

**Table 3.5:   Direct Marketing Full-Service Agencies Based on Estimated U.S.
Gross Billings
(in millions)**

Agency	Billings	
	1980	1981
Young & Rubicam (Wunderman, Riccota & Kline; Stone & Adler; Chapman DM)	$142.0	$166.7
Ogilvy & Mather Direct	38.7	55.6
Rapp & Collins	27.4	36.5
Smith, Hemmings, Gosden	20.9	22.7
Compton Direct Marketing	20.0	23.5
TLK Direct Marketing	19.0	20.0
Kobs & Brady Advertising	18.7	21.5
The DR Group	14.6	20.5
MARCOA	12.0	13.0
Soskin/Thompson	9.8	19.6
N.W. Ayer	9.3	17.7
Grey Direct	7.2	11.2
Ketchum, Macleod & Grove	5.0	7.0
Throckmorton/Zolfo	3.5	4.5
J.W. Prendergast	2.8	3.2

Note: This list represents those agencies who responded to our request for data.

Source: *1982 Fact Book on Direct Response Marketing* (New York: Direct Marketing Association, Inc.), p. 7. Reprinted with permission.

thermore, direct marketing organizations have repeatedly demonstrated a determined willingness to make use of these advances. In an international study conducted by DMA in 1980, direct marketers were asked to list the most important technological developments in their countries relative to their businesses. Three developments were especially important: computers, ink-jet and laser printing and viewdata telephone systems. Computers can be used today for market research, list maintenance and sophisticated segmentation of prospective buyers. Computerization of these functions gives direct marketers flexibility and response capability that did not exist with manual systems. Ink-jet printing is used for mailing labels and for adding personalized information to an offer. Viewdata (videotext) is being used increasingly (mostly outside the U.S. at this time) to link customers directly to organizations that have goods and services to offer.

At the same time, telecommunications has played a key role. The telephone is widely used today for direct marketing. WATS lines ("800" numbers) are used extensively for both incoming and outgoing calls between consumers and direct marketers. AT&T offers discounts for WATS lines based on volume usage. Consumers are encouraged to contact direct marketers on WATS lines since calls can be made toll free (to the caller at least). Few direct response offers today, which involve long distance toll calls, are made without including a toll-free "800" number for customer use.

The use of credit cards issued by banks, financial service organizations and retailers has become widespread, thus establishing instant credit for millions of consumers and facilitating direct response purchases on a widespread basis. It is doubtful if direct marketing would be growing so rapidly without the credit card networks that are in place today.

The message is clear: direct marketers have a tradition of early adoption of new technology, and this attitude will likely be a decisive factor in their willingness to pioneer the use of videotext, teletext, cable and video discs.

DIRECT MARKETING ON CABLE

Marketers have long used television to air direct response ads, often tied into toll-free ("800") telephone numbers. (The "not-available-in-any store" direct response TV promotions are all too familiar to television viewers.) Most of these promotions have found their way to independent stations where they are usually aired outside of prime time on a "preemptible" basis (run only if a time slot is not filled by "regular" commercials). For broadcasters, most direct response ads are looked upon as a necessary evil: they fill unsold advertising time not purchased by "regular" sponsors.

As cable has increased its penetration, direct response advertisers have looked to it as a partial replacement for broadcast television, whose rates have increased and whose time availabilities have been reduced. Furthermore, cable offers longer play time for direct response ads since it is not restricted, as is broadcast TV, by the FCC, which limits the number of minutes per hour that can be allocated to commercials.

However, the cable networks are beginning to look askance at direct response ads much as the independent broadcasters have done. They accept such ads, usually on a preemptible basis, but their primary objective is to attract sponsors of products and services that are recognized by the public, and many direct response products do not meet that criterion.

Ted Turner's super-station, WTBS, has been among the most aggressive of the cable networks in seeking direct response ads, and so has CNN, the Cable News Network, also a Turner programming venture. However, WTBS has been cutting back on direct response ads as regular advertising has increased.

The cable shopping show format is a sort of continuous direct response TV commercial, which promotes products as entertainment and allows viewers to respond by telephone. Cable has the potential to go much further than the cable shopping show format. Cable technology has not progressed to the point where highly selective transmission is possible in most areas, but eventually it will be able to deliver or "address" ads to target viewers much as direct mail or magazines do now. Some targeting will be possible with one-way addressable technology, which some systems are now installing for pay-per-view programming. However, full-scale targeting will only become possible with the installation of two-way capability, a task that will take at least five years to reach a high level of penetration. When this happens, cable use for direct response advertising should gain considerable momentum.

At that point, cable operators could become more interested in cable direct response, if they were offered economic incentives. This could be done if advertisers were willing to pay commissions for all viewer responses that are directed by viewers through the cable system. In fact, operators will probably insist that this type of fee be paid. The next chapter discusses electronic marketing on cable in detail.

DIRECT MARKETING ON VIDEOTEXT AND TELETEXT

Videotext, teletext and direct marketing appear to be converging for a number of reasons. First is rising costs, both of traditional direct marketing methods which include creative work, production, supplies and promotion, and of postage. Third class rates for bulk mailings more than quadrupled from 1960 to 1979; today postage can represent as much as 25% of the total cost of a single mailing. The substitution of electronically published material for printed matter begins to make sense as the cost of direct mail continues to rise.

Second, timing and flexibility must be considered. Offers made via printed material require a great deal of time to prepare and distribute. Sometimes an offer is partially out-of-date by the time it is actually received by the consumer. Electronic means can substantially reduce the amount of time from the concept stage to the actual offer. Consequently, the offer can be made timely, reflecting immediate conditions. Print offers can be changed but only at considerable time and expense and only if an early feedback mechanism is in place and is working effectively. It is much easier and more practical to make changes electronically.

Advantages and Disadvantages of Videotext

The advantages and disadvantages of videotext in direct marketing are summarized in the following list. They are presented in detail in Chapter 5.

Advantages

- Can be adapted to cable or telephone transmission (the latter gives it potential for universal coverage).

- Has an unlimited data base which can be continuously updated.

- Extensive cross-referencing of data base information is possible.

- Full two-way capability makes shopping and banking from home or office possible.

- Can be merged with payment system mechanisms (credit and debit cards) to facilitate transactions.

- Ideal for extensive listings, directories, schedules that change frequently and must be consulted prior to a purchase (travel, entertainment, etc.).

Disadvantages

- Perceived as "computer-like" and thus too complicated for the ordinary consumer.

- Initial costs to establish networks for system operators and information providers (computers, data processing, communications, etc.) are high.

- Initial hardware costs (adapters, decoders, modems, keypads, personal computers, etc.) are high.

- Requires ongoing fixed subscriber fees and variable transaction fees.

- Visual displays provide limited space (compared to print) and do not have moving video or audio (like television).

- Not portable.

- Hard to browse.

Finding the Offer

When used for direct marketing, cable channels, videotext and teletext are unobtrusive to consumers. They are quite different from print offers, catalogs and similar materials, which are mailed directly.

Data bases can include several hundred thousand pages of information, and a viewer must find his way to any offers that exist in the vast amount of material on file. How can a consumer be expected to find a specific offer out of hundreds of thousands of pages that could be stored on a videotext system?

Compounding the problem is the fact that electronic terminals are not portable in the sense that a printed document is. Since terminals lack portability, will people be inclined to use them to search for offers? Marketers will have to develop innovative methods to encourage people to check their electronic mail slots for the latest offer directed to them.

One way of doing this would be to offer economic incentives. The consumer might be credited a small amount if he consulted a specific offer, and a larger amount if an actual purchase were made. Another method would be to tie in a videotext offer with other media. The consumer could be alerted to the offer by a ''blurb'' on teletext, cable, television, radio, or in a newspaper or magazine or on a billboard. Moreover, the videotext service could establish a special TV directory which consumers could periodically check for the availability of specific offers.

Economic Considerations

The cost of establishing videotext services and of using them will give pause to service providers and consumers alike. Until there are a sufficient number of homes with videotext/teletext receivers in use, traditional direct mail marketing will be cheaper and more effective than electronic marketing (see Chapter 5).

Despite the high start-up costs, businesses, in their search for cost reduction and in their fear of being left behind competitors, are likely to take up the cause of new technology. This pattern is already quite apparent in the financial services industry, which has invested heavily in automated equipment such as Automated Teller Machines (ATMs) and which has just started to do the same in home banking systems.

How much consumers are willing to pay, on what basis and how much can be expected from advertising are all critical questions that have yet to be answered.

However, some answers are expected to begin emerging from videotext trials conducted by Time Inc., Knight-Ridder Newspapers, Inc., American

Telephone and Telegraph Company, CBS/AT&T, The Times Mirror Company and Cox Communications. The U.S. telephone system is based on usage-sensitive pricing over and above a small monthly service charge. The cable industry bases its pricing on flat fees to subscribers although pay-per-view program fees will become an exception to that strategy. It is expected that electronic marketing services will combine flat fees with specific transaction costs. Flat fees could include a portion of the hardware (decoders, keypads, modems etc.) costs which are expected to remain high for two-way services until high production levels for equipment can be reached.

In the U.S., electronic transactional systems have not moved to the point where realistic pricing strategies could be put to the test. Some figures could begin to emerge from the Knight-Ridder Viewtron service scheduled for 1983. Knight-Ridder has announced that it will charge subscribers a flat fee of $25. (After the 1980 Coral Gables Viewtron test, subscribers had said that they would find the service useful and that they would be willing to pay for it in the future.) Whether additional fees will be assessed is not yet known. The British approach of usage-sensitive pricing will probably not sell in the U.S. where fixed rates or "tiered" pricing is more acceptable for services of the type that are planned.

CONCLUSIONS

Direct response selling methods in electronic marketing are merging to provide new segmentation techniques to reach many different publics, such as consumers, voters, contributors and so forth. Direct response selling has grown much more rapidly than conventional retailing over the past decade, due to many factors discussed in this chapter. This trend is expected to continue as mass markets and advertising, supported largely by broadcast TV, decline in efficiency due to media fragmentation. Furthermore, the new electronic media, which are going through their initial struggle for financial support, will turn increasingly to direct response, for it is here that they can supply applications that are commercially justified.

4

Cable, Teletext and Other One-Way Electronic Marketing Systems

For electronic marketing to become successful in the U.S. its developers must fill three roles: they must plan and operate telecommunications and data processing networks; they must supply and package services and information in an appealing and economical manner; and they must provide affordable hardware to system operators and consumers.

A few organizations are sufficiently diversified to fill more than one role, but more often, an individual firm will not be able to go it alone. Consequently, organizations with complementary skills and resources will form alliances to offer services to the public. The trend is already evident in a number of videotext trials: American Telephone & Telegraph Company and Knight-Ridder Newspapers, Inc. offering Viewtron; AT&T and CBS Inc. offering Venture One; the Cox Cable Communications affiliation with HomServ and ViewMart, subsidiaries of American Can Company, offering Indax; and Keycom Electronic Publishing, formed by Field Electronic Publishing, Centel (Central Telephone & Utilities Corporation) and Honeywell Inc.

PLANNING ELECTRONIC MARKETING SYSTEMS

The framework for electronic marketing in the U.S. is beginning to develop, but caution is the watchword. Many organizations involved in development do not adopt long-term plans, but instead pursue immediately achievable programs that can be implemented through existing operations. This attitude is consistent with the short-term, bottom-line mentality that has seized American management and has seriously throttled innovation.

Both one-way and two-way systems are being developed for electronic marketing. This chapter offers a detailed discussion of one-way systems;

Chapter 5 deals with two-way systems. Table 4.1 provides a summary of the key elements of both systems and their major characteristics.

It should be pointed out that arbitrary distinctions run the risk of over-simplification. Eventually elements of one system may be merged with elements of others. Some features may become predominant and others may disappear completely. In general, as shown in Table 4.1, one-way systems are simple to design, easy to operate, economical for the user and available today. Two-way systems are more complex than one-way, cost more to establish and operate and are either in the trial stage now or in an early phase of commercial development.

Table 4.1   Characteristics of Electronic Marketing Systems

Systems	Characteristics
One-way Cable Crawl Direct Response Services Shopping Channels Teletext	Easy to operate Technically simple Little or no additional cost to operate Supported by advertising Provides limited information Has two-step transactional capability Competes directly with other media such as newspapers, radio and TV Requires no additional equipment and can be operated on regular TV (teletext is an exception, requiring a decoder)
Two-way Time-sharing Videotext	Some instruction required to operate Technically more complex Requires substantial hardware costs Supported by advertising, subscriber and information provider fees Can provide unlimited information Has interactive or one-step transactional capability Can be distinguished from print media. More like online catalog or directory Requires a personal computer and related equipment, or relatively expensive equipment to adapt a regular TV

Source: Compiled by the author.

ONE-WAY SYSTEMS DESCRIBED

One-way systems can be divided into two major categories. The first is "printed video"—text only or text and graphics displays without sound or moving video. Automatic origination services, classified ad channels and teletext all fit into this category. All of these services are a form of electronic marketing since they can carry advertising, and in the case of classified channels, they are advertising. The second category of one-way systems is conventional television (moving video with sound), which is used to deliver direct response ads. A variation is the cable shopping channel, which is programming devoted exclusively to direct response commercials.

By inserting a telephone number for viewer reply, all of these services can be used in a two-way mode. However, until links are established that allow computerized interaction between buyers and sellers, full two-way capability will not exist. The Qube system in Columbus, OH, is a step in that direction. Qube gives viewers the ability to order merchandise. However, the approach was all-or-nothing. Viewers, on command, could order by pushing a button, but that was all they could do. There was no way that a dialog could be established, as can be done with a human operator on a telephone or with a data base accessed by personal computer or videotext terminal.

AUTOMATIC ORIGINATION SERVICES

Over half the cable TV systems in the U.S. supply automatic origination text services which are satellite-fed to them by major wire services such as the Associated Press or United Press International. In some cases the service is offered by a local newspaper either in conjunction with the cable operator or on a leased basis. These services provide headline news, sports, weather reports and program listings, often accompanied by background music from an FM station. They are sometimes referred to as "crawl" or "scroll" services since the text appears one line at a time just as it would on a typewritten page.

A major shortcoming of this type of service is that the display, being limited to text, lacks visual appeal. Furthermore, the user has no interactive control over the information that comes across the screen. These systems, however, have introduced millions of viewers to the idea that the TV set can be a source of textual information. Nevertheless, the whole concept of using TV for anything but entertainment and "live" news is foreign to most viewers.

CLASSIFIED AD CHANNELS

Classified ads are a major revenue source for newspapers throughout the nation. According to figures released by the Newspaper Advertising Bureau, in 1981 classified ads reached $4.7 billion out of a total $17.6 billion spent for all newspaper advertising.

With revenues of this magnitude the newspaper industry is determined not to let this valuable franchise slip into the hands of outsiders such as the cable or telephone industry. Newspaper interests were successful in blocking AT&T from testing its Electronic Information Service (EIS) in Austin, TX, in 1981. EIS would have evaluated AT&T's ability to collect, organize and disseminate information electronically. The newspaper industry regarded this activity as a clear threat to its role in publishing and advertising.

Several services or trials that distribute classified advertising electronically by telephone or cable have been conducted or are underway. They include the Associated Press on CompuServe; Leader TeleCable, publisher of the Eau Claire, WI, *Leader Telegram,* which has offered a classified service on a local cable system; Televised Real Estate, a service on cable systems in California and Washington; and Manhattan Cable TV, Inc. in New York City, which offers its own classified service.

With the exception of CompuServe, there is no interaction between viewers and ads, which run sequentially much like a text service. Most people who consult classifieds have a good idea of what they are looking for. Thus, they want "on-demand" capability so that they can immediately zero in on what is of interest. Services that do not offer such a capability will probably not meet with broad acceptance. Nevertheless, electronic classifieds on one-way systems will not disappear. Many newspapers will perpetuate them to protect their franchises. However, in the long run, two-way services will be more appropriate for classified channels since they will provide the interactive capability that users need. (A more detailed discussion on classified advertising is in Chapter 6.)

TELETEXT

Teletext is a one-way system capable of delivering text and graphics to an ordinary TV set equipped with a decoder. Transmission can be on broadcast or cable TV. Teletext offers a TV "newspaper" which furnishes news headlines, sports information, weather reports, highway conditions, information on community events, entertainment listings and the like. The ability to update information continuously makes teletext a "real-time" information service. Teletext can draw on local, regional and national sources for the information that it provides.

Teletext "frames" or pages are created on special equipment and stored in a computer data base for transmission to viewers. The technical side of organizing, operating and maintaining the system has many similarities to that of videotext. The creation of pages and the editorial process are closely related to activities in the newsroom of a newspaper, thus making teletext a close relative of newspapers. Material prepared for a newspaper must be reformatted for transmission by teletext, but eventually preparation will involve only one step. Teletext ads can be full screen or anything smaller. Most are expected to be one-liners, appearing at the bottom or top of the page.

A broadcast teletext signal is sent "piggyback" fashion on the unused portion of a TV transmission known as the vertical blanking interval (VBI). Teletext signals are transmitted in digital form. These signals are run through a special decoder, attached to an ordinary TV, which converts them to the text and graphics displays that the viewer sees on his screen. For technical reasons, broadcast teletext is limited to several hundred pages at most. Teletext delivered by cable uses full channel transmission; that is, an entire channel is dedicated for this purpose. Consequently, cable systems can handle several thousand pages of material. Viewers with teletext sets will be equipped with small keypads that will enable them to grab and hold pages in the transmission cycle. When this is done, regular programming disappears from the screen but the sound can be retained.

Teletext Planning

The jury is still out as to what the "ideal" teletext system might eventually look like. The fact is there may not be such a system. The determining factor in the selection of a teletext system will be the type of operation already in existence, with broadcasters opting for over-the-air transmission and cable operators choosing full-channel service. Broadcasters will be the first to jump into teletext service since they can do so for a relatively modest investment. Many have already conducted teletext trials, the most prominent of which are discussed in this section. However, cable transmission cannot be overlooked. Time Inc. is currently in the lead in the development of teletext for cable.

Advertising will be an integral part of teletext. It will have to become the mainstay of financial support since it is unlikely that viewers will be willing to pay for such services. The advertiser's ability to update messages on a continuous basis should benefit consumers by making them instantly aware of late-breaking changes. Teletext advertising could also direct users to other information sources such as print media or videotext for additional details on items of particular interest.

For broadcasters, however, teletext advertising will be a problem for two reasons. First, many broadcasters fear this new technology will tempt the viewer to "browse" through the electronic information service during regular commercial breaks. Diverting viewers away from regular commercials has become an increasingly sensitive issue for agencies, advertisers and broadcasters with the proliferation of new media forms. Pay TV and video cassette recorders (VCRs) are currently the biggest contributors to audiences being diverted from regular commercial programming. Teletext and videotext are expected to create additional diversions.

Second, broadcasters suspect that advertising expenditures on teletext will cut into regular advertising budgets. It is unrealistic to figure that the dollars spent on teletext will be additional expenditures over and above what is normally planned for regular broadcast advertising. The same problem holds true for newspapers who establish teletext services. Reader diversion may not be such a big problem, but there could be an impact on regular advertising revenues as sponsors switch some of their funds from print to electronic media.

The exact cost of delivering teletext depends on many variables, such as the transmission mode and the extent of editorial support. Walter Cicioria, director of product marketing, Zenith Radio Corporation, has indicated that a cable operator would need a monthly subscriber fee of $6 to break even. This calculation is based on cost assumptions of a 25% royalty for information providers, a $180 decoder, a 20% interest rate and a five-year payback. Cicioria believes that a $2 to $3 monthly cost is within striking distance as decoder prices fall and if interest rates do the same. However, as previously stated, teletext services will have to figure out a way to cover such costs from advertisers, since subscribers are unlikely to pay for information which essentially can be obtained for nothing from existing media.[1]

Teletext Trials

Commercial teletext service has been operating in Great Britain since 1976. The BBC's version is known as Ceefax and the Independent Broadcasting Authority (IBA) offers Oracle. By mid-1982 there were some 300,000 sets equipped to receive teletext transmissions in Great Britain, with an estimated 50,000 sets reaching the market monthly. The French and Canadians have also developed teletext technologies known respectively as Antiope and Telidon. A number of teletext trials have been conducted in the U.S., all using foreign technology. All of these services have included electronic marketing in the guise of advertising and infomercials

---

[1]Based on an article in *Multichannel News* (March 15, 1982), p. 7.

sponsored by retailers, publishers, travel organizations and so forth. A brief description of the most prominent trials follows.

CBS and NBC

CBS Inc. was at the center of a teletext trial, launched in April 1981 in Los Angeles, which ran until late 1982 and which included the following participants: The CBS/Broadcast Group; Station KNXT, the CBS-owned and operated station in Los Angeles; the National Broadcasting Company, Inc., Station KNBC in Los Angeles; the Caption Center (for hearing impaired) of WGBH-TV Boston; public station KCET; and Télédiffusion de France, developer of the Antiope hardware used in the test. KNXT, KNBC and KCET published separate teletext "magazines." The CBS version, Extravision, featured approximately 80 pages of news, sports, weather reports, stock market and financial information, flight information, traffic conditions, entertainment listings and the like. KCET's electronic magazine, Now!, focused on science, finance, films, public affairs, medicine and content for young viewers. Initially 20 teletext-equipped receivers were placed in public locations such as schools, museums, department stores and shopping malls. One hundred in-home terminals were later placed throughout the Los Angeles area. CBS is getting ready to launch a nationwide teletext service, which would be transmitted via satellite to its affiliated stations. This service is expected to start in early 1983 although the FCC had still not authorized commercial teletext by the end of 1982. The NBC service, known as Tempo NBC Los Angeles, provided viewers with about 100 pages of material such as news headlines, sports information, weather reports and traffic conditions. NBC has announced that it, too, plans national teletext service starting in 1983.

NBC, CBS and KCET, in an unusual display of cooperation, all plan to share the research data gathered from the Los Angeles trials. This information was scheduled to be made available to the participants by the end of 1982.

Cable Teletext

Cable delivery systems for teletext using full channel transmission are being offered by two companies. Keycom Electronic Publishing (KEP) in a joint venture with Satellite Syndicated Systems (SSS) is already in operation and an unnamed service is being tested by Time Video Information Services.

The KEP and SSS venture has produced the Keyfax National Teletext Magazine. KEP is the result of a three-way venture including Centel Corporation (54%), Honeywell, Inc. (30%) and Field Enterprises, Inc. (16%). The venture is a good example of the pooling of resources, discussed in Chapter 2, to exploit new electronic media opportunities. Eventually, it is KEP's plan to offer both teletext and videotext service.

Keyfax was first tested by Field Electronic Publishing on Chicago Station WFLD in conjunction with a sister division, *The Chicago Sun-Times*. The trial used material from the paper which was reformatted prior to transmission. The five categories of material offered to trial sets included news headlines, sports, finance and business, weather and traffic reports and entertainment listings. Figure 4.1 shows the Keyfax general index page. In addition to teletext transmission, Keyfax was offered on a full-channel basis during nighttime hours when the station would have otherwise been off the air.

In November 1982, Keyfax was offered nationally to cable systems. The signal is transmitted on the vertical blanking interval (VBI) of superstation WTBS by SSS, a common carrier based in Tulsa. Subscribers must pay a $25 installation fee and a $19.90 monthly service fee which includes a leasing charge for a decoder and keypad. Under the present revenue sharing arrangement, the cable operator receives only $3.95 a month, with the balance going to Keyfax and the equipment manufacturer. The long-range goal is to sign up some 220,000 homes by 1985 (about 1% of WTBS' total

Figure 4.1: Keyfax general index page. Courtesy KEYCOM Electronic Publishing; copyright 1983. Reprinted with permission.

reach at the end of 1982). Subscription income will have to be the revenue mainstay for the near term, but advertising revenue would become predominant over the long run if everything goes according to plan.

Despite its intention to carry advertising, Keyfax had not published a rate card when it went national. Doing so is rather impractical when you have so few viewers. Keyfax has some other rather serious barriers to hurdle when it comes to attracting advertising support. Since it is a broadcast service, it is limited to 100 pages. Furthermore, there is no provision for local information or ads to be inserted. Thus, until local content can be merged, Keyfax must offer itself as a national service only, and this could turn out to be a real drawback to acceptance by cable operators and subscribers alike.

Time Video Information Service, Inc., a subsidiary of Time Inc., is also offering a cable teletext service, but its strategy is entirely different. Time has created a teletext magazine that has 14 "content clusters" on some 5,000 pages including news, sports, financial information, games, puzzles and entertainment guides. The service will be satellite distributed to cable systems. A full-scale trial was launched in late 1982 in 400 homes in two American Television and Communications (ATC) cable systems located in San Diego and Orlando. ATC is a Time subsidiary.

Time has made provisions for local input, which will be supplied primarily by newspapers. Initial plans call for an $8 to $12 monthly subscription fee. However, advertising will be carried and should eventually become the major source of revenue.

Time has gone to great lengths to encourage participation by advertising agencies during the early stage of development. It has formed an advertising advisory council consisting of six major agencies. They will each pay a modest fee to participate, and they will create and test ads for their clients.

Testing should continue in 1983, and national rollout is expected by 1984 if early results prove encouraging. Time is obviously modeling the teletext service after its highly successful pay TV service, Home Box Office (HBO), in that it is a satellite-distributed, subscription service in which cable operators can share revenues. However, here the similarity ends, since teletext is text and graphics TV rather than a familiar entertainment form such as motion pictures.

Despite the high risks involved, Time is one of the few companies that could make the service work and that is willing to invest the millions of dollars required over several years to get the project off the ground.

The prospects for teletext as an electronic marketing vehicle seem rather limited. Assuming that decoder costs can be reduced to levels that do not discourage subscribers from purchasing teletext-equipped sets, teletext penetration will be modest over the next five years or so. Where the real problem lies is in consumer acceptance. The question is, will there be sufficient consumer use to encourage advertisers to invest in teletext ads. This is impossible to answer now, and current research efforts may reveal only meager and even deceptive clues to the future. The answer will only come by trying it out on a wide enough scale to be meaningful. Obviously such an approach carries risks. It also requires a commitment from TV manufacturers, who have the capacity to incorporate decoders into sets before they leave the factory. The market for such sets cannot be expected to take off until the cost to consumers of teletext-equipped sets represents only a small additional expense. Manufacturers are currently talking in terms of $150 to $200 for decoders. Anything more than a $25 differential could be a problem. Clearly, economies of scale at the manufacturing end are needed.

MOVING VIDEO AND AUDIO TV PRESENTATION

One-way services are also used for advertising through conventional techniques using moving video and audio. This is the type of advertising that people are accustomed to watching, having been exposed to it for so many years on broadcast TV.

However, cable offers new possibilities for advertisers. It does not labor under the rules that apply to broadcasting concerning the length, content and the amount of advertising that can be run. Furthermore, there are many channels to be filled with programming. Direct marketers are trying to figure out ways to use them effectively to reach cable subscribers, who are generally believed to be better-than-average sales prospects, based on their demographic make-up.

Two forms of direct marketing that have already appeared on cable are direct response ads and cable shopping channels.* The first is a carry-over from broadcast TV, which has always run direct response ads but which has given them "stepchild" status. Regular ads, whose sponsors are usually well-known to the public, are favored by TV space salespeople over direct response ads promoting lesser or unknown products. The latter often create a less than respectable image in the minds of wary viewers. Cable shopping channels represent a sort of nonstop direct response ad in that an entire show is programmed as an ad. Both formats display a telephone number which viewers can use to order merchandise or services directly. This is the best that can be done today using one-way cable.

In the future, as two-way systems proliferate, viewers will be able to interact with merchants and service providers at the touch of a button. Their response will be carried to a computer by cable or telephone lines

---

*For information on shopping channels, the author is indebted to Leslie Grey, senior editor, *Home Video and Cable Report*.

where their order will be recorded and billed automatically with no delays, no busy signals and no dealing with uninformed telephone operators.

Suppose they are not ready to order, but need more information. Two-way systems will accommodate them. By pushing another button, a request for information on an advertised item will be registered. This information could be delivered by conventional mail (if the viewer doesn't mind an interminable delay) or instantaneously by electronic means, for a small fee, to those viewers equipped with a personal computer or its equivalent. For the next few years, however, most cable systems will be limited to one-way service with telephone response possible. It will take time for the direct response ads and cable shopping channels of today to evolve into the more advanced two-way systems of the future.

Direct Response Services

Direct response advertising has run on broadcast TV for many years. Its commercials are targeted to specific viewing groups who are encouraged to respond by calling a number flashed on the screen. Direct response TV commercials put heavy emphasis on such products as books, records, tapes, small appliances, vacation properties and personal services. Most direct response TV commercials are relegated to stations looking to fill up unsold advertising slots during fringe viewing time. This policy puts serious restrictions on when and where direct response ads will run. They could find new success on cable where abundant channel capacity is open to them.

Two examples of direct response advertising on cable are "The Video Shopper," which was launched on a regional basis in late 1981, and WATS (Wide Area Telephone Service) Marketing of America, a national direct response affiliate of American Express. These services buy time primarily on cable networks to run their direct response commercials.

"The Video Shopper"

"The Video Shopper" was created by American National Cable Communications, Inc. (ANCCI), an independent marketing firm. The service, which features housewares and electronics, initially ran 30- and 60-second local spots on two cable networks, Entertainment and Sports Programming Network (ESPN) and Cable News Network (CNN), using Cablevision Systems of Long Island, Viacom of Central Islip, NY, and Gill Industries, in the San Jose, CA, area. The original service was launched in September 1981. In addition, ANCCI mailed a catalog with some 260 items to selected cable subscribers. The commercials and catalog em-

could contact to place orders. Fulfillment of orders was handled by Consumers Distributing Company, a catalog showroom operation, where customers could go to pick up merchandise they had ordered.

Results of the original service were poor. The cable systems had limited reach and few audience research data were made available, thus making it difficult for sponsors to buy time on the service.

In early 1982, ANCCI planned several changes, including shifting the service to superstation WTBS, which is metered by A.C. Nielson and which is the number one cable network, with a reach of over 20 million homes. Distribution was to shift from Consumers Distributing to direct shipments from the manufacturers via United Parcel Service. However, the change to WTBS did not materialize, and the future of "The Video Shopper" is uncertain at this time.

WATS Marketing of America

WATS Marketing of America has been active in bringing clients, including its parent, American Express, to broadcast TV. It is now offering its service to cable networks on a per-inquiry basis. Clients do not pay a fixed rate for their direct response commercials; rather, they pay based on the number of inquiries that any specific commercial generates. Each participating network is assigned a different "800" toll-free telephone number. WATS Marketing has offered to furnish its clients with demographic data free of charge as an inducement to use the service.

Shopping Channels

Cable shopping channels represent an approach to marketing that was never tried on broadcast TV, since channels were too scarce to be dedicated to this activity. Shopping channels are TV programs dedicated to selling goods and services, a concept that originated in the early 1970s. Programming was designed around "live" demonstrations of products in a way that would have entertainment value. Viewers could make an inquiry or place an order by calling a number displayed on the screen. Some well-known names in the retail field, such as Neiman-Marcus, were involved at an early date.

Early attempts did not work out for several reasons. First, cable penetration at the time was much lower than it is now. Second, satellite transmission was not available, which meant that programming was limited to local markets. Program distribution depended on the physical delivery ("bicycling") of video tapes to individual cable systems, a method that is not very efficient.

On a shopping channel, a sponsor buys time segments that can run as long as a half hour. In some cases, professional actors are hired and scripts are prepared. In others, the program involves what can be described as an enhanced commercial. An intensive product demonstration is programmed for the segment, which will usually be repeated a number of times over a one- to two-month period. A number of these services are either operational or have been tested. Table 4.2 lists the major cable shopping channels.

Table 4.2   Selected Cable Shopping Channels

Service (Owner)	Cable Outlet	Status	Date Begun
"Home Shopping Show" (Modern Satellite Network)	Modern Satellite Network (MSN)	To be reactivated in March 1983	1980
"The Shopping Channel" (Times Mirror Cable and Comp-U-Card of America)	Times Mirror Cable	Terminated after trial	1981
"The Winning Shopper" (Comp-U-Card of America and Metromedia)	Unknown at this time	Will not run on CBN Satellite Network as originally scheduled	—
"The Cableshop" (Adams-Russell Cable and Soskin-Thompson Associates/J. Walter Thompson)	Adams-Russell Cable	Operational	1982
"The Shopping Game" (American Video Shopper)	Satellite Programming Network (SPN) and 19 independent systems	Off the air	1982
"The Cable Store" (The Cable Store)	Unknown	Off the air	1982

Source: Knowledge Industry Publications, Inc., and the author

phasized demonstrations and comparisons of competitive items within a product category. Both included a toll-free number which readers/viewers

"Home Shopping Show"

The "Home Shopping Show" was originated by Washburn Associates, a Chicago advertising agency. It was subsequently acquired by Modern Satellite Network (MSN), a basic cable network with a reach of some 4 million households. Originally sponsors took 8½-minute segments, but the service later accepted 30-second and 60-second spots. MSN has billed the "Home Shopping Show" as cable's "foremost consumer information service." After many format changes, the show was running for a half hour, five times a week. Toward the end of 1982, the "Home Shopping Show" was removed for a face lift. It is scheduled to return in March 1983 as a half-hour weekly show. Figure 4.2 shows a cooking scene from the "Home Shopping Show."

"The Shopping Channel"

"The Shopping Channel" was a joint venture of Times Mirror Cable, the nation's sixth largest MSO, and Comp-U-Card of America, a privately held company and the operator of the Comp-U-Store electronic shopping service. (Comp-U-Card's operations are described in Chapter 5.) Federated Department Stores, Inc. holds a 10% interest in Comp-U-Card. This investment is significant in that it represents one of the first commitments by a retailer in electronic marketing, even though Federated's involvement is decidedly indirect at this point.

"The Shopping Channel" was distributed on a trial basis during 1981 via satellite to six Times Mirror Cable franchises, serving 150,000 subscribers. The program schedule ran seven days a week for 16 hours a day. Program segments for each promotion ran for 30 minutes. Viewers could call a toll-free number to make inquiries or to place orders through Comp-U-Card's facilities. Purchases could be made using a major credit card. However, shoppers were required to become members of Comp-U-Card by paying an $18 annual fee.

"The Shopping Channel" was not continued beyond the planned 4-month trial period. Officials of both companies have refused to comment on the results of the trial. The reasons for the end of the Comp-U-Card/Times Mirror venture are not clear. Rumor has it that personality conflicts at both the personal and corporate level had as much as anything to do with the divorce.

Figure 4.2: The "Home Shopping Show" offers consumer information and demonstrations as well as products. Courtesy Modern Satellite Network.

"The Winning Shopper"

Comp-U-Card has since formed a joint venture, Shopping by Satellite, with Metromedia, a major independent broadcaster, to offer a shopping channel. Known as the "The Winning Shopper," the service was scheduled for distribution on the CBN satellite network. However, those plans have been dropped, and the future status of the shopping channel is uncertain.

"The Cableshop"

Advertising and cable interests have joined forces to create "The Cableshop," a service that airs commercials that subscribers have requested by calling a toll-free number. "The Cableshop" is a joint venture of Adams-Russell, a Peabody, MA, cable system (8,000 basic subscribers) and Soskin-Thompson Associates, the direct marketing subsidiary of J. Walter Thompson. The 52-channel system is using three channels on a 24-hour-a-day basis for the service. A fourth channel is used as a program directory. Although the system has interactive capability, it is not used for "The Cableshop" service.

When the service was launched in March 1982, more than a dozen JWT clients had been signed up for a trial run, including Scott Paper Company, Reynolds Metals Company, Arrow Shirts, Franklin Mint Corporation, Campbell Soup Company, Prudential Insurance Company of America and Ford Motor Company.

"The Cableshop" is unique in that it is a "video-on-demand" advertising service rather than a scheduled program. Viewers consult the directory channel and can then use a special telephone number to request a specific advertising "message," which is specially prepared for the service and runs for three to seven minutes. After requesting a specific message viewers must wait at least several minutes before it plays, a delay that could discourage use.

The "Cableshop" test has been running since March 1982. Plans now call for expanding to six markets by July 1983. Soskin-Thompson is expected to play an active role in the test by tying in direct mail and print advertising to support the service.

"The Shopping Game"

The ubiquitous game show, which is used by local stations to fill prime time that the networks are prohibited from programming, has been emulated by "The Shopping Game." Created by American Video Shopper, a cable and television direct marketing service, "The Shopping

Game" was a 30-minute show that aired in 350 cities on Satellite Programming Network (SPN), a cable network. The program offered its products in a game-show format, concentrating on such items as tool sets, electronic products, cameras and expensive housewares, which could be ordered by calling a toll-free number. There were also opportunities to win vacation trips, by mailing in a postcard or a coupon provided by the cable operator.

"The Shopping Game" has been terminated, and its future status is uncertain.

"The Cable Store"

"The Cable Store" was a shopping show that opened in June 1982 in the Dallas/Fort Worth area and soon expanded to other cities in Texas, Alabama, Florida, Virginia and South Carolina.

The service did not discount prices. It specialized in books, toys, kitchen items and travel products, ranging in price from $7.50 to $260. Viewers could order merchandise using a toll-free telephone number and paying with credit cards. Items were shipped by United Parcel Service for a small shipping charge.

"The Cable Store" ran eight hours a day in Dallas and in one-hour segments repeated four times daily in other areas.[2] The program was terminated in December 1982.

Additional Shopping Channels

New shopping channels are certain to emerge. Indications are that ABC Video Enterprises and Warner Amex Satellite Entertainment Corporation (WASEC) could both enter the field. WASEC has already announced plans for such a service, which would be launched in mid-1983 on one of its new cable systems in either Houston or Dallas. By that time, it is anticipated that its Qube service would be improved to the point where transactional capability, including placing of orders, is possible. First generation Qube was actually used for shopping during the Christmas season of 1979. Because each Qube subscriber is "polled" by computer, the user could place an order by touching a button on his keypad when instructed to do so by an announcer.

The Via-Tel Corporation of Massachusetts is planning Video Mail Order service for early 1983. VMO's 60-minute segments will feature products from 50 mail-order houses, such as Carroll Reed Ski Shops, Stur-

---

[2]Information on "The Cable Store" from *Home Video and Cable Report* (March 22, 1982).

bridge Yankee Workshop and the Chesapeake Bay Trading Company. Customers will place orders using a toll-free telephone number.[3]

Prospects for Shopping Channels

The widespread use of shopping channels in their present form does not appear imminent for a number of reasons. First, since broadcasters have no spare channels, the appropriate vehicle for carrying shopping channels is cable TV. However, there are two drawbacks to using cable. Cable systems will be reluctant to turn valuable channels over to a shopping service when they can use them for highly profitable entertainment programming such as pay TV. This is especially true for the more than 40% of cable systems that still have fewer than 13 channels. Furthermore, cable's projected penetration, even if the most optimistic figures are to be believed, will never exceed 55 to 60% of all households in the U.S. This level of penetration could be viewed as a limitation by sponsors accustomed to universal reach on regular broadcast TV. The success of shopping channels on cable TV will depend on the demographics of the audience that actually watches and uses them.

Second, the economic return of shopping channels is not well known at this time. Sponsors face two cost components: In most cases they must pay for air time—services with long advertising or demonstration segments operate on this basis. The second component is production cost of the product demonstrations. Production costs vary widely and depend upon complexity, locale, number and salaries of actors used, equipment involved and so forth. With viewer expectations generally rising with respect to TV quality, shopping channels are faced with the prospect of having to invest substantial sums to make their presentations stimulating, informative and professional. A shopping channel has to compete with the "pure" entertainment programming that it is trying to emulate.

Third, shopping channels are linear rather than interactive. They are not capable of producing information "on demand" as a videotext or video disc service can. "The Cableshop" comes closest of all, since viewers request specific advertising information, but it cannot be considered interactive. Most people do not have the time or inclination to sit down and watch a long series of product demonstrations in the hope that they will come across something that interests them. They want immediate access to specific product information.

Finally, shopping channels must deal with the issues of order fulfillment, billing, follow-up service and product liability, just as any retailer or

---

[3]*Home Video and Cable Report* (May 3, 1982).

direct marketing organization must. Merely offering products and services on television is not enough. It is impractical for a shopping channel to accept such responsibilities, but if it does not, it must then assign them to suppliers. Furthermore, customers must understand who is responsible for what, and even more important, they must have confidence that any problems connected with placing an order or with the merchandise received will be resolved expeditiously.

CONCLUSION

Both categories of one-way service will play an increasing role in electronic marketing. Text and graphics services will be used, although sparingly, for certain types of advertising that tie in with these essentially information-oriented delivery formats which people will glance at fleetingly between more intensive sessions with their TVs.

"Regular" television presentation, which includes moving video and audio, holds greater promise. Conventional advertising on cable networks has fallen far short of expectations. Thus, unique approaches employing direct response techniques will be promoted as alternatives. However, the full potential of direct response services and cable shopping channels will not be realized until two things happen. First, two-way cable and telephone capability are needed to make responding as easy as possible. Second, this type of advertising will have to be skillfully coordinated with other advertising and promotional vehicles including videotext, video discs and different types of print media.

5

Time Sharing, Videotext and Other Two-Way Electronic Marketing Systems

Two-way electronic systems are more complex, harder to use and more expensive than one-way systems. However, two-way means interactive—systems that allow the user to request specific information and to conduct transactions from a computer terminal or an adapted TV set. On balance, the potential of two-way systems for electronic marketing is substantially greater than that of one-way systems, for reasons that will be explained in this chapter.

TIME SHARING

Time sharing developed in the 1950s and 1960s largely in response to government and military needs to access large amounts of information on computers. By the early 1960s, there were many computer installations that allowed over 100 users to "time share," or simultaneously interact with the same computer. Later, as time sharing became popular for commercial users, it also became the primary means of delivering online data bases to researchers, librarians and corporate users. Throughout the 1970s, time sharing remained the domain of specialists who knew how to query the data base.

In the late 1970s, organizations such as Dow Jones, The Source and CompuServe recognized that the same telecommunications and computers could be used to deliver information to businessmen, professionals and consumers, whose purchases of personal computers provided a new market. Data bases most likely to be of interest to the general public, such as news, financial information, home shopping, travel guides and airline schedules, were introduced. At the same time, simpler ways of searching the data bases were implemented, particularly the use of menus or directories instead of keywords or commands.

It can be argued that the distinction between time-sharing and videotext systems is an arbitrary one. They both are communications systems that link subscribers to electronic data bases. However, time-sharing systems were created to serve commercial rather than consumer markets. Although some time-sharing services are taking steps to reposition themselves, their primary focus will continue to be on business, professional and institutional users. Videotext systems, on the other hand, are based on hardware and software that can serve consumer as well as businesses.

The data base of a time-sharing system may consist of proprietary contents and of material acquired from outside sources for resale. The system operator is usually a publisher or data processing operator who, in effect, becomes an electronic publisher of the different services included in the data base. Many data base producers who formerly sold services only through proprietary distribution to specialized information users now have a means to expand their markets by affiliating with a time-sharing system operator who can resell their material.

Subscribers in many cities can call up the system with a local phone call. They then use their terminals to communicate directly with the data base of the time-sharing service over telephone lines or packet switching networks. Users are charged for connect time on a rate schedule that usually offers discounts during nonbusiness hours. Some of the services offer transactional capability by connecting subscribers to third-party computers (gatewaying). Table 5.1 provides a summary of the three major time-sharing services, which are described in more detail in the following sections. Although there are many other time-sharing services, the three discussed here most closely resemble consumer services, though their primary orientation is still business use. Also included is a description of Comp-U-Store, an electronic shopping service that has many of the characteristics of a time-sharing system.

CompuServe Information Service

The CompuServe, Inc. information retrieval system was introduced in 1979 as MicroNET, a designation that was later changed to CompuServe Information Service (CIS). CompuServe is primarily a data processing service and formed CIS to get greater utilization of its computer facilities during evening and weekend periods, when business use declined sharply.

Users of personal computers or data terminals can subscribe to the service, which offers information and entertainment options, including the

Table 5.1:   Major Time-sharing Services for the Consumer Market

Service	Number of Subscribers	Hourly Connect Fees (Range)	Transactional Services
CompuServe Information Service (H&R Block)	34,000	$6-$15	Electronic banking (through Financial Interstate Services Corp.) Electronic shopping
Dow Jones News/ Retrieval Service (Dow Jones and Co., Inc.)	54,000	$9-$72	Electronic shopping available through premium cable service
The Source (Readers Digest)	25,000	$6-$26	Electronic shopping available through Source Plus, a premium cable tier

Source: The author; prices approximate.

following: news summaries from the Associated Press, *The Washington Post* and Canadian Press; a financial information package called FINTOL; video games; literary and movie reviews; electronic mail service; and personal computing aids. Electronic banking is available through a gateway to Financial Interstate Services Corp., Shawmut Bank of Boston or Huntington Bank of Columbus, OH. Electronic shopping is possible through Comp-U-Store (see below). Two recent additions are the World Book Encyclopedia (offered by a subsidiary of Scott and Fetzer, Inc.) and the Official Airlines Guide; both services are accessed through gateways.

The CompuServe data base can be accessed by a local phone call in some 260 cities across the country. Transmission between local cities and CompuServe's computers in Columbus, OH, is by a private leased line. Plans also call for cable hookups through CompuServe's INFO channel, a system designed for interactive cable; although INFO is now available it is not currently being offered by any cable operators.

CompuServe subscribers pay an initial sign-up fee, plus hourly usage fees of $15 during regular business hours and $6 during off-peak periods. Subscriptions can be arranged either directly with CompuServe or through Radio Shack, which acts as a dealer for the service. By late 1982, 34,000 subscribers had signed up, most of them in the business and professional category.

Although its consumer information retrieval business is growing, CompuServe still obtains most of its revenue from its corporate time-sharing business. It will be a number of years before revenues from information retrieval services account for a significant share of overall revenues.

Dow Jones News/Retrieval Service

The Dow Jones News/Retrieval Service is an information utility offering financial and business data. As of late 1982, the Dow Jones service had 54,000 subscribers. Over 70% of these are corporate accounts. Information can be accessed by telephone, using a personal computer or data terminal.

Of the three time-sharing services discussed in this section, Dow Jones is the least consumer oriented. It offers consumers the Home Information Retrieval Service, which includes the News/Retrieval Service, an electronic encyclopedia and other news data bases, some from outside sources. Radio Shack is involved as a dealer for the service, which can be accessed through its TRS-80 computers.

The News/Retrieval Service is also available on two-way cable systems. Subscribers can lease the equipment necessary to access the service on cable for about $15 a month. Rather than paying for connect time, the service is offered on a tiered or fixed-fee basis. A basic tier for $12 is available during nonbusiness hours. A premium tier costing $50 provides full-time access to the News/Retrieval Service and a full range of data base services as well as teleshopping services, for which subscribers are switched (or gatewayed) to Comp-U-Store. Like most information providers to the home market, Dow Jones needs partners who can offer complementary services, such as Comp-U-Store, in order to offer consumers a diversified package.

Home services using cable have already been tested on two suburban systems in Dallas, and additional tests are planned at various locations around the country, including a cable system in Princeton, NJ, co-owned by Dow Jones. The cost of terminals and headend, or transmittal, equipment is considerable. As a result, Dow Jones may have to underwrite or subsidize franchises to get the program rolling.

The Source

The Source Telecomputing Corporation was founded in 1979; the Reader's Digest Association now owns a controlling interest in it. By the end of 1982, The Source had managed to sign up over 25,000 subscribers, who pay an initial cost of $100 and between $6 and $26 an hour for con-

connect time, depending upon the hour when the system is used. Users can communicate by telephone, using a personal computer or low-cost terminal to access over 50 data bases and more than 1400 specific services. Source Cable is available to cable TV systems with a limited number of data bases. Its most prominent exposure is as a participant on the Cox Cable Indax system. Source Plus is an enhanced service offered as a second tier. It includes Media General (stock analysis), Commodity News Service, Management Contents (business publication abstracts) and Legislate (a weekly tracking service of congressional legislation activity). Subscribers to Source Plus can be connected to Comp-U-Store.

The origins of The Source are quite different from those of CompuServe Information Services and Dow Jones News/Retrieval Service, which grew out of existing businesses looking for ways to expand. The Source was created from scratch, spurred largely by the boom in small computers. However, like the other time-sharing services that are trying to become more consumer oriented, The Source still concentrates on the business and professional market.

Comp-U-Store

Unlike the time-sharing systems just described, which are essentially broad-based information utilities, Comp-U-Store is a service dedicated exclusively to electronic shopping. However, from a functional standpoint, it is similar to time sharing, in that Comp-U-Store subscribers must use personal computers or low-cost terminals, and they must use the same search and retrieval procedures that are used for the diversified time-sharing services.

Comp-U-Store is a service offered by Comp-U-Card of America. In 1973, Comp-U-Card offered its telephone shopping services to large corporations as an employee benefit. Participating organizations either underwrote or sponsored Comp-U-Card memberships for employees, who could dial a toll-free number for price information on easily recognizable, brand-name merchandise. If a desired item was available, the member could check to see if Comp-U-Card's price was lower than the suggested price of local retailers. (The customer could still deal with the local merchant, who had the option of matching or beating Comp-U-Card's quoted price.) Eventually Comp-U-Card expanded beyond corporate accounts by offering individual memberships. The service has now grown to over 2 million members. Although Comp-U-Card receives a commission of from 3% to 5% from suppliers for any item that it sells directly to a member, the bulk of its revenue is derived from annual membership fees, which run between $18 and $25, paid by corporations on behalf of employees or by individuals on a direct basis.

Comp-U-Card is strictly a telephone service. Comp-U-Store, which was launched in 1981, is a primitive but fully electronic shopping service. Using a personal computer, a Comp-U-Store subscriber can be connected to the Comp-U-Card data base, which includes 19 categories of band-name merchandise, including clothing, jewelry, cameras and major appliances. Subscribers pay a $25-per-year membership fee plus $5 to $18 an hour for connect time, depending on the time of day. In addition, subscribers to The Source or CompuServe can access Comp-U-Store and can place orders using a major credit card. When gatewaying to Comp-U-Store, subscribers pay only the regular connect time fees charged by the underlying service, but they must hold a membership in Comp-U-Store.

Use of Comp-U-Store requires a personal computer, which limits the number of people who can subscribe to it. Any orders that are placed must be forwarded by Comp-U-Card to the appropriate supplier. Despite these drawbacks, Comp-U-Store is certainly a first step to full teleshopping service, where consumers will be able to communicate and place orders directly with suppliers rather than going through an extra off-line step.

Comp-U-Store's real value at this time is as an electronic directory to the information stored in the Comp-U-Card data base. Those who know how to use a personal computer can browse through and compare price and product features, thereby saving time and money.

Comp-U-Card is developing two other services that will operate from its data base. Comp-U-Claim, now operational, is used by insurance claims adjustors to obtain replacement costs for lost, stolen or damaged merchandise. The proposed Video Comp-U-Store will allow retailers to order merchandise from the Comp-U-Card data base using an instore terminal, which can be connected to a video disc for product presentations. Although Comp-U-Card is privately owned, investors include Federated Department Stores, Inc., Equitable Life Assurance Society of the United States, Merrill Lynch & Co., Inc., Reader's Digest Association, Inc. and the Jack Eckerd Corporation.

Disadvantages of Time-sharing Services for Electronic Marketing

Time-sharing services leave much to be desired for use in electronic marketing. For the typical consumer they are not "user friendly." They are primarily designed as information retrieval systems for business and professional people who are familiar with operating a computer or other types of terminals. While the lack of graphic capability and color displays is not a problem for information services, it is a serious drawback in marketing products that depend on visual appeal. Furthermore, time sharing via telephone uses a pricing strategy that relies on connect time fees.

Consumers will be reluctant to use electronic systems for transactional services if charges are time sensitive. They are more likely to accept fixed subscriber rates combined with transaction fees, as offered on cable systems. However, while the telephone system reaches virtually every consumer in the nation, cable reaches only 30% of all households. Two-way cable, the type required for time sharing, is only in its infancy, and it will be many years before it reaches enough households to make time sharing via cable commercially feasible.

Although future developments will probably be in other electronic media, the time-sharing systems available today have provided some valuable insights and information for the future of the consumer market, including hard data on operating and marketing costs. They have also clearly proved that much more marketing must be done to extend such services beyond the narrow base of early adopters.

VIDEOTEXT AS A MEDIUM FOR ELECTRONIC MARKETING

Videotext is a two-way communication system that resembles time sharing in a functional sense but is designed to be operated by practically anyone, using a television set, a telephone or cable connection and a low-cost decoder. Videotext systems do not rely on a personal computer or its equivalent. Figure 5.1 shows the process of selecting a product offered on Telidon Videotex Systems.

Development and Testing

In Europe and Canada, videotext has moved to an advanced stage of testing and early commercial development, assisted in most cases by generous infusions of capital from governments anxious to exploit the technology both domestically and in foreign markets. Videotext in the U.S. has yet to go beyond the early trial stage. The focus of trials conducted to date in the U.S. has been mostly technical, to test computers, communications systems, terminals and peripheral equipment. The current trials, which started in the 1981-1982 period and will run through 1984-1985, are expected to probe issues related to long-term consumer acceptance.

Although development in the U.S. has been slower than elsewhere, the tempo is accelerating. U.S. development is still hampered by lack of a cohesive national effort, but it is unencumbered by technological axes to grind. Unlike France, Britain or Canada, the U.S. has no indigenous technical standard—except for AT&T's presentation level protocol (PLP) —that it is pushing for adoption. By entering the contest late, the U.S. has been able to select technology developed elsewhere, as a customer, rather

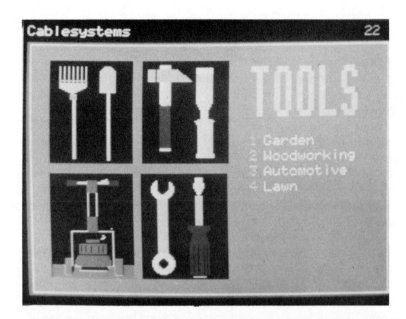

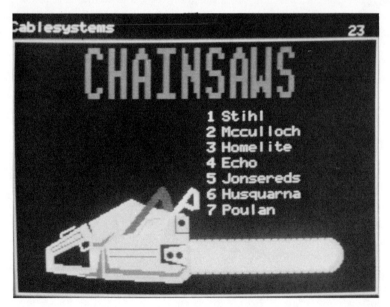

Figure 5.1 The shopper selects the category "tools" (top) and is then given a selection of several different brand names (bottom).

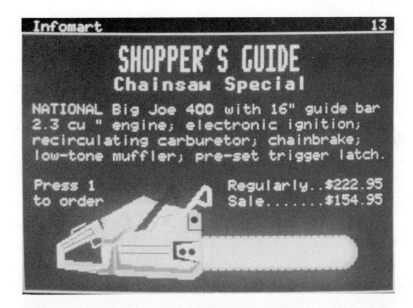

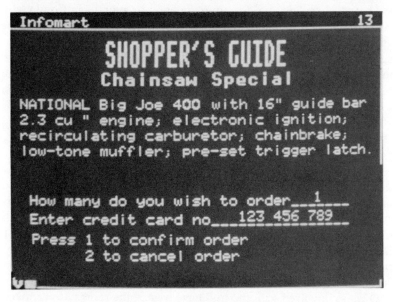

Figure 5.1 (continued) Once the shopper chooses a brand, a description of the product is given (top). The system then provides the shopper with the opportunity to place an order (bottom). Courtesy Telidon Videotex Systems, Inc.

than as a vendor. The question of technical standards is discussed later in this chapter.

Development in the U.S. also reflects the complexity of making videotext happen. Of the three key roles that must be fulfilled—system operation, service/information provision and hardware supply—few if any organizations can do it all. This is why videotext is making strange bedfellows as alliances, joint ventures and cooperative arrangements have started to proliferate. An increasing number of videotext trials can be expected between now and 1985. Based on projected rates of acceptance and anticipated investment in hardware and software, large-scale commercial operations cannot be expected until some time after 1986. What follows is a discussion of the major U.S. trials that have been completed, are underway or are planned.

Viewtron

The most prominent U.S. videotext trial to date has been Viewtron, conducted jointly by AT&T and Viewdata Corporation of America, a subsidiary of Knight-Ridder Newspapers, Inc. The trial, which cost an estimated $2 million, ran for approximately six months in Coral Gables, FL, in 1980-1981. Knight-Ridder provided much of the software support and coordinated information and advertising. There was no charge to advertisers or participating homes. AT&T supplied 30 home terminals, manufactured by Western Electric Company, Inc., and managed communications. The terminals were rotated among 160 Coral Gables homes to study consumer attitudes and interest in using a videotext system. Over 10,000 pages of information and advertising were made available to viewers. Viewtron pages were an alphanumeric presentation with color, enhanced by Prestel-type alphamosaic graphics.

Information providers included *The Miami Herald,* Consumers Union, *The New York Times,* Dow Jones, Associated Press, CBS Publications and others. Advertisers consisted of both national and local concerns. Among the national group were Eastern Airlines, Inc., Sears, Roebuck & Co., B. Dalton Co., Merrill Lynch & Co., Inc., J.C. Penney Co., Inc. and Service Merchandise Co., Inc. Local advertisers included a bank, a supermarket, a travel agency, a record dealer, a boat equipment distributor, a realtor, a liquor store and a ticket agency.

Officials involved with the trial have treated the results as proprietary. Nevertheless, Viewdata Corporation of America has announced plans for a commercial launch reaching 5000 homes in South Florida in 1983. Subscribers were not charged during the 1980-1981 trial, but a $25 monthly fee has been proposed for the commercial service. Such a charge should aid in determining real demand. In addition, Knight-Ridder has announced agreements with other publishers whereby it will share market research results. This suggests that Knight-Ridder could embark on a franchising or joint venture strategy. Companies named so far include Capital Cities Communications, Inc. (owner of *The Kansas City Star/Times, The Star-Telegram* of Forth Worth, TX, and Fairchild Publications, Inc.) and Affiliated Publications, Inc. (owner of *The Boston Globe*).

Viewtron's emphasis in the trial was on information. Knight-Ridder perceived itself as a packager of information—from both internal and external sources—that could be transmitted to consumers. Although videotext research has not yet yielded much substantive data, there seems to be increasing evidence that information by itself is not enough for the consumer market. The experience of Prestel in Great Britain would seem to prove that a more diversified package must be offered to attract a large number of subscribers.

To remedy the lack of appeal inherent in systems that rely heavily on information, Viewtron will have to offer enhanced transactional capability. In the trial, Viewtron users were able to shop for goods and services from participating advertisers. However, although orders could be placed and paid for by using a credit card, they then had to be relayed offline to the vendors by Viewtron. For the 1983 service, Southeast Bank (Southeast Banking Corp.) will be included as a service provider offering home banking, but it is not clear what steps are being taken to improve teleshopping.

Cox Index

Cox Cable, a subsidiary of Cox Broadcasting Corporation, is the nation's fourth largest multiple system operator (MSO), with more than 1 million basic subscribers. During the 1980-1981 period Cox was particularly successful in gaining new franchises in Omaha and New Orleans, among other cities. It has the distinction of operating the nation's largest franchise, located in San Diego, with 211,000 subscribers.

Cox Cable has always excelled from an engineering standpoint. It has placed great emphasis on the development and installation of state-of-the art equipment. Unlike most of the cable industry, it has supported two-way technology, and it has persisted in its development despite enormous costs and a series of delays and setbacks that would have discouraged most companies. This strategy inspired the development of its proprietary two-way interactive system known as Index, an acronym standing for INteractive DAta eXchange. Like Warner Cable's Qube system, Index has attracted a great deal of publicity and attention as a "system of the future," well before its economic viability can be demonstrated based on operational experience. Nevertheless, Indax is capable of delivering full video-text service, something that Qube cannot do.

An Indax trial had been scheduled for early 1981 in 300 San Diego homes. However, a series of technical problems forced a delay. This trial finally got underway in spring 1982. Despite the delay, Cox still had plans to install Indax in its Omaha, New Orleans and Vancouver, WA, systems in the 1982-1983 period and to make retrofits in existing systems located in Santa Barbara, CA, and Macon, GA, when they are rebuilt.

Indax trial homes are supplied with a small keypad and a micro-processor adapter, which convert the home TV to an Indax terminal. Subscribers are able to retrieve information from local data bases and from The Source, and they can perform banking and shopping trans-actions. Cox's strategy calls for offering Indax as a tiered service: subscribers will pay a monthly subscription charge for the basic package, plus additional fees for transactional services based on actual usage.

Banking services for Indax have been designed and will be supported by HomServ, a subsidiary of Fingerhut Corporation, the direct marketing division of American Can Company. Shopping services will be supplied by Viewmart, also a subsidiary of Fingerhut. HomServ and Viewmart will be responsible for applications software, and they will serve as middlemen between the cable system and merchants and banks connected to the system. Subscribers using HomServ will have a choice of banks that they can use. Transactional fees will be shared by Cox, HomServ/Viewmart and participating banks and merchants.

Indax's reliance on cable could present a problem. People who use the system for transactional purposes would have difficulty if they want to switch to merchants and service providers outside the system. Switching would require hybrid connections to combine cable with telephone or possibly other cable systems. The technical and engineering complexities are significant, as are the agreements that would be required between different cable organizations and between the cable and telephone industries. It remains to be seen if coordination of this type will actually be achieved. Telephone transmission systems do not face this obstacle.

Videotex America

The principal business of the Times Mirror Company is newspaper publishing. Its major newspapers are *The Los Angeles Times, The Dallas Times Herald, Newsday, The Hartford Courant* and *The Denver Post.* The company is also extensively involved in broadcasting and cable TV. In late 1982, Times Mirror Cable ranked as the ninth largest MSO with close to 740,000 basic subscribers.[1] Times Mirror has been extremely aggressive in pursuing opportunities related to cable. In 1981 it formed Times Mirror Satellite Programming. Also in that year, it formed Spotlight, a proprietary pay TV service and linked up with Comp-U-Card of America for purposes of testing The Shopping Channel on some of its cable systems. (That service was not continued beyond the original trial period.)

In 1982 Times Mirror Videotex Services, Inc., a subsidiary of Times Mirror, formed a joint venture with Infomart, itself a joint venture of Southam and Torstar, two Canadian publishers. The new venture, named Videotex America, is responsible for the development and promotion of Telidon in the U.S. It has already signed an agreement with Phoenix Newspapers, Inc. to explore possibilities for a videotext service. This type of agreement could be a model for tie-ins with other newspapers, a prospect that is also being pursued by Knight-Ridder Newspapers.

Early in 1982, Videotex America launched a trial that includes 350 southern California homes. Telidon reported that it was supplying a complete system under an initial contract worth over $1 million. The trial includes 70,000 pages of news and information from *The Los Angeles Times,* the Associated Press and other publishers; retail and classified ads; airline flight schedules; Ticketron service; and consumer information. Advertising is being tested and will be supplied by retailers such as Carter Hawley Hale Credit Corporation, The Broadway department store, Sears, and Waldenbooks. Transactional services will include banking offered by Bank of America and electronic shopping service offered by Comp-U-Store. A more extensive test, which could include up to 2,000 homes, is planned for 1983.

Venture One

CBS, Inc. and AT&T have joined forces to offer a videotext trial in approximately 200 Ridgewood, NJ, homes. This trial was launched in late 1982 and is expected to continue into the spring of 1983. The service, which has been unofficially dubbed Venture One, offers 8000 pages of the standard assortment included in videotext trials, including news, information and games. In addition, teleshopping and home banking will be tested. Sixteen advertising agencies and 80 of their clients are also participating to test various types of advertising on videotext.

Users will be able to order merchandise by using an electronic order form appearing on the screen or by using an automatic telephone dialer

---

[1]*Home Video and Cable Report,* November 22, 1982.

linking them to the advertiser. The trial will be more of a concept test and technical evaluation than anything else, but it does bring together two major participants who eventually figure to play major roles as electronic marketing develops.

FirstHand

In December 1981, First Bank Systems, Inc. announced that it would establish a videotext system for information, banking and shopping services. The test was noteworthy because it was the first U.S. banking trial to use the French videotext technology and because it chose a relatively specialized audience, agribusiness, which is an important market for First Bank Systems.

FirstHand, as the service was known, had a test base of more than 250 terminals in areas of North Dakota and in Minneapolis/St. Paul. Customers could make a local phone connection to the system, which provided agribusiness bookkeeping systems, weather, commodity and financial reports and news. Banking services included funds transfers between accounts, bill paying and balance information. Users could also play video games and purchase products from participating retailers. Tymshare, Inc. provided technical support, including private telecommunications between Minneapolis and the other test areas.

The trial has been completed, and the future of this service is unknown at this time.

WILL VIDEOTEXT SUCCEED?

Transactional Capability

The ability to conduct transactions for products and services will be essential if videotext is to succeed. Early results have proved that information alone is not attractive to many consumers—unless they are using it for business or professional purposes. The British found this out the hard way when Prestel failed to draw large numbers of consumers. (Of course, there were other reasons for Prestel's slow start, which are discussed later in this chapter.)

Videotext operators in the U.S. who are serious about penetrating the consumer market will have to include transactional services. There are two ways that this can be done: network files can be replicated and maintained separately from the provider and updated on a regular basis, or a network can be designed with the ability to switch or "gateway" users directly to the provider's files, providing online transactional capability. Unfortunately, both procedures are costly and complex to set up and operate.

Videotext Graphics

The British and French systems use alphamosaic displays. In this type of presentation the graphics are chunky or "chairstep" in outline. By contrast, Telidon, the Canadian technology, uses an alphageometric display, which produces smoother edges and a higher resolution image. Figure 5.2 shows how each system would display a picture of Albert Einstein. Higher resolution has provided Telidon with a competitive edge in the battle for acceptance in some of the current trials outside of Canada.

Although Telidon's superior graphics have been considered important in providing a realistic display of products, there is conflicting evidence on consumer demand for this capability. Yankee Group, a Cambridge, MA, consulting firm, surveyed a group of media and marketing executives for their preference on display protocols. The respondents favored either simple text with alphamosaic graphics or full video to alphageometric display.[2]

To complicate this issue, a more recent study contradicted the Yankee Group findings. Reymer & Gersin, a research firm, recently reported that consumers appeared inclined to pay more for a videotext service with high resolution graphics. This finding is based on results released from Reymer & Gersin's National Home Electronics Test, a study run in 16 cities during the summer of 1982. Obviously the jury is still out on the graphics issue.

However, despite its importance from a strictly cosmetic standpoint, graphics have not necessarily been the key consideration in the selection of a given technology. In many cases the decision has been based on expediency. Operable equipment at the right cost has been hard to come by. As a result, availability at the time of a scheduled field trial was often the decisive factor rather than consideration of graphic capabilities.

Technical Standards

Outside the U.S., technical standards have been established by government fiat, and each nation is competing fiercely to have its standards adopted in overseas markets. In the U.S., the Federal Communications Commission (FCC), which frequently intervenes in standard-setting procedures for broadcasting, has remained on the sidelines, favoring resolution by the marketplace.

Teletext Standards

For teletext, both the British standard and the French standard have their supporters. A modification of the French Antiope system comforms

---

[2]From Yankee Group's syndicated subscription research series "Home of the Future."

Figure 5.2 The difference in graphic representation systems is illustrated by the alphamosiac simulation (top) and the alphageometric display (bottom). Courtesy Telidon Videotex Systems, Inc.

to the North American Broadcast Teletext Specification (NABTS) standard, which is being supported by CBS and NBC and will be used on their national teletext services. Those supporting the British standard point out that it requires the lowest investment of any system offered. Critics maintain that it is also the least diversified technology.

Videotext Standards

For videotext, an equally fierce battle is emerging. Some have supported the British Prestel standard, but most others prefer a North American Standard that emerged from AT&T's Presentation Level Protocol (PLP) announced in 1981, with which the French and Canadians claim compatibility. That standard has been modified after much discussion, and an agreement could be reached between U.S. and Canadian groups supporting a standard referred to as "Presentational Level Protocol Syntax" (PLPS). Meanwhile, 26 European countries have agreed on videotext /teletext standards developed by CEPT (European Conference of Posts and Telecommunications).

Importance of Standards

There is a real difference of opinion as to how important international technical standards might be to the long-range development of videotext and teletext. Those in favor of such standards claim that they would make the job of equipment manufacturers easier and that they would bring down equipment and software costs faster. Others, however, point out that the television industry already operates with different standards for North America, Europe and Japan. International technical standards may be more important to manufacturers outside the U.S., who must develop export markets if their large investments in videotext and teletext technology are to pay off.

The result of this indecision has been a hesitant and fragmented effort in the U.S. private sector. Industry, which is unsure of the demand for videotext/teletext service, seems ready to exploit the best elements of foreign technology through licensing arrangements or by purchasing turnkey systems, thereby avoiding the obvious risks of developing its own technology. Nevertheless, application of foreign technology does not settle the standards issue, since French, British and Canadian systems are all being used in U.S. trials, and they are not totally compatible. Until this matter is resolved, broadcasters, hardware manufacturers and software providers will not go forward as fast as they might. No one wants to make significant investments in technology that may not ultimately be accepted in the marketplace. Without standardization, hardware manufacturers may not achieve the economies of scale that would make terminals affordable for the mass public.

Despite a late start in testing new technologies and an inability to agree on standards, the U.S. should eventually catch up with other countries in the application of new media for electronic marketing. However, the technologies will have to compete among themselves, with market forces providing a sort of "natural selection" process. Undoubtedly, by choosing standards in this way, the acceptance of electronic marketing will take longer than it would have if standards had been governmentally imposed.

Forecasting the Market for Videotext

Estimating the growth of videotext has become a favorite pastime for consultants, researchers and the like. Trying to gauge the possible acceptance by users of a new medium that is not entertainment driven is extremely difficult. The number of households subscribing to videotext and teletext is subject to wide variances depending upon who provides the figures. Based on what is known today, significant penetration cannot be expected prior to the late 1980s. However, by the early 1990s, an acceleration in videotext and teletext usage can be foreseen. Table 5.2 provides a 10-year forecast indicating that by 1993, 30 million homes could be using videotext and teletext.

The annual expenditure in dollars for videotext service is also a subject for much speculation. However, if only 10 million households become subscribers by 1993 and they pay an average monthly fee of between $10 and $30, annual revenues would run between $1.2 and $3.6 billion, as

Table 5.2:   10-Year Forecast of Videotext and Teletext Subscribers (millions)

	1983	1988	1993
TV households	85.6	94.5	104.2
Cable households	30.0	44.0	55.0
Two-way households[1]	5.0	20.0	26.0
Videotext households	0.1	2.0	10.0
Teletext households[2]	—	4.0	20.0

[1]Includes homes passed by two-way cable, two-way telephone and hybrid systems
[2]Includes broadcast and cable transmission

Source: Compiled by the author for "Advertising Applications for the New Electronic Media," a report for International Resource Development, Inc., Norwalk, CT, February 1983.

demonstrated in Table 5.3. This estimate represents the subscriber fee only. To this must be added additional sources of revenue such as installation fees, sale or rental of hardware, frame access fees, frame creation and storage fees, transaction fees and advertising. How much additional revenue these would produce is anyone's guess, but it could be many times the amount represented by subscriber fees. Advertising itself could run from $2 to $3 billion if classified and electronic Yellow Page directories are included. It is quite evident that videotext has the potential to become a multibillion-dollar-a-year industry.

Table 5.3: Estimated Annual Revenue from Videotext Subscriber Fees (in billions)

Number of Subscriber Households	Monthly Household Subscriber Fee						
	$10	$15	$20	$25	$30	$40	$50
7,500,000	$0.9	$1.35	$1.8	$2.25	$2.7	$3.6	$4.5
10,000,000	$1.2	$1.8	$2.4	$3.0	$3.6	$4.8	$6.0
12,500,000	$1.5	$2.25	$3.0	$3.75	$4.5	$6.0	$7.5

Source: The author.

Economic Considerations

For businesses who want to reach consumers, the rising costs of traditional marketing methods are forcing a determined search for alternatives. Although the conversion to electronic methods produces savings in cost of printed material or television commercials, these savings must be compared to the offsetting costs of creating, storing and distributing videotext and teletext offers. Britain's Prestel system is the only working model of a commercial system. Information providers must pay an initial registration fee, frame creation costs and frame storage fees. The average annual cost to create and maintain a single frame on Prestel runs between $50 and $75, to which some portion of the registration fee must be added.

The consumer could be the biggest stumbling block. Again, the British model can be invoked. Subscribers to Prestel, Ceefax or Oracle must have special equipment to allow their TV sets to receive videotext or teletext. This equipment includes a decoder and keypad or an alphanumeric keyboard. For videotext, a modem is also required so that signals can be transmitted back and forth on the phone line. This additional equipment can add as much as $400 to the overall price of a TV set. Although this figure has dropped considerably in the past two years, it is still high enough to be a barrier to mass market penetration. This is one of the major reasons why Prestel has not been successful with consumers in Britain.

In addition to hardware, which is a one-time cost, Prestel subscribers must pay for the telephone call that connects them with the computer, the connect time that they are actually on the system and frame access charges, which can vary from as little as 2 cents to as much as $1 depending upon what the information provider elects to charge.

Advantages of Videotext and Teletext

Since videotext and teletext are computer based and rely on advanced telecommunications, they have a number of advantages for direct marketing. First, videotext is the only medium, except the telephone, which has the capability to combine an offer with an immediate response. This added convenience for consumers holds the potential for increased sales by the marketer, since the tendency to respond on impulse to an offer is increased if there is a convenient way to do so. Videotext also provides the ability to slice markets into minute segments. The computer makes it possible for the marketer to carry on a continuous rejuggling of the market segments that are of interest. The communications element of videotext allows the direct marketer to transmit his offer to different market segments as quickly as they are identified by the computer.

Second, since videotext is computer based, it can be tied in with the computers that most direct marketers aleady use for maintaining mailing lists and processing orders. This tie-in offers many advantages. Computer capability allows rapid analysis of consumer buying behavior, and the response to an offer can be measured accurately and instantaneously in real time.

Third, not only can messages be precisely targeted to specific customer groups, they can also be personalized, based on buyer behavior profiles held in the computer. Of course, the dark side to having such information available is the danger of invading consumers' privacy. This is an issue that the new electronic media have only just begun to address. Some sketchy attempts at self-regulation have begun to appear. Warner Amex Cable Communications Inc., for example, has announced a self-regulating code that would be used to protect the privacy of its subscribers against unwarranted intrusion.

Videotext also has real benefits for consumers. It permits direct dialogs between a consumer and a merchant or service provider in a far less cumbersome manner than by telephone or mail. Furthermore, such dialogs can be established at any time of the day or night, 365 days a year. Information, directories and catalogs can be accessed with an ease and flexibility that is practically impossible by other means. A high degree of comparison and cross-referencing is possible, making the shopper better informed than he ordinarily would be about a product or service.

In effect the consumer can create his own direct marketing information package based on his individual requirements. This can be done on demand rather than by waiting for a specific offer to be transmitted. Thus, the consumer gains a measure of control over what he is willing to look at and when he will actually do the looking. The implications for direct marketers who are used to controlling the timing of the interaction will be substantial. Discrete offers transmitted on a scheduled basis will give way to a continuous flow of information, which consumers will be able to access whenever they sit down at a terminal connected to a videotext or teletext network.

Disadvantages of Videotext and Teletext

There are a number of problems with using videotext and teletext for marketing. They present stumbling blocks that will slow the adoption of these technologies for direct marketing.

The amount of text that can be delivered on a screen is limited when compared to printed material. This limitation means that videotext and teletext material has to be sent in summarized form. Extensive detail cannot be shown unless several screens are linked together. Of course this presents the risk of losing the viewer who tires of glancing from one screen to another to gather all the details that he is looking for.

Pictorial presentation is another problem, as discussed earlier in this chapter. Many products must have at least color still-photo (called alphaphotographic) capability if they are to be offered on videotext or teletext. The systems available today use computer generated graphic displays. Picture-like presentations, while within the state of the art, are currently being done only on an experimental basis. Furthermore, there will probably be additional costs to create and transmit them. In many cases, even still-photo presentation will be inadequate. Nothing short of moving video with sound will do. None of the trials or commercial videotext systems that are running or planned have such an advanced capability. (It is rumored that Time Inc.'s teletext trial could incorporate sound.) The task of weaning people from their dependence on photographic visual displays could be a real problem for offering products on videotext and teletext.

The ideal format would combine the best qualities of print with the speed, flexibility and interactive qualities of electronic publishing forms. What is needed is the broadband capability of cable, the universal switching capability of the telephone and the large-screen presentation that projection television will be able to deliver. Until all these pieces come together, direct marketing on videotext could be limited to products and services that do not require a high level of presentation quality. A partial solution will be for consumers to use print catalogs with an electronic system as a supplement, which could update information in the printed version.

SUMMARY

Two-way systems that provide electronic marketing capability are in their infancy, and it seems that many factors are conspiring to hold back their acceptance. Time-sharing services offered by Dow Jones, Compu-Serve and The Source Telecomputing are black-and-white alphanumeric systems based on information retrieval for business and professional subscribers. They were never designed for transactional purposes.

At the next level, a number of videotext trials are either planned or underway. They have been created by publishers, broadcasters and telecommunication organizations, who are just beginning to test the market for electronic services offered to consumers. Today there are more questions than answers about the ultimate acceptance of these services.

The success of cable TV, pay TV, VCRs, video games and personal computers proves that consumers are willing to pay for new electronic delivery systems. However, these systems are used almost exclusively for entertainment. Electronic marketing is another matter. Its success will depend on low-cost, easy-to-use systems with clearly demonstrable benefits. Nevertheless, after a slow start, videotext and teletext could well reach 10% and 20% respectively of all households in the U.S., thus opening up possibilities that are little more than hopeful ideas at this time.

6

Advertising Using
the New Electronic Media

Advertisers have traditionally searched for ways to reach large numbers of people, mostly through mass media—newspapers, magazines, radio and television. The new electronic media, however, suggest possibilities that move away from large, consolidated audiences. Cable TV, video cassettes, video discs, teletext and videotext are media for reaching specialized, fragmented market segments. This chapter evaluates the potential of these media for advertising, with special emphasis on videotext.

Reaching specialized audiences is a common feature of the new electronic media and has particular importance for direct marketing, as was discussed in Chapter 3. Other features of the new media are quite different, as Table 6.1 shows, and suggest different possibilities for applications in electronic marketing.

CABLE TV

Cable TV, of all the emerging new media, has attracted the most attention—both in publicity and actual dollars invested by advertisers. The growing interest in cable as an advertising medium is due in great part to its popularity as an expanded form of TV. However, Madison Avenue has been slow to embrace cable programming as an advertising vehicle because any one program reaches only a small fraction of the audience that networks reach, and methods to measure the size and composition of audiences are still primitive. Additionally, the biggest audiences on cable are those watching pay TV, which has been off limits to advertisers. Nevertheless, advertisers' resistance to switching some buys to cable is declining.

Estimates for the growth of cable TV advertising vary widely. A middle-of-the-road projection offered by Link Resources Corporation, a New

Table 6.1:   New Electronic Media—Comparison of Features

	Inter-active	Update Capability	High Storage Capacity	Audio	Moving Video	Graphics Capability
Cable TV	No[1]	Yes	NA	Yes	Yes	NA
Video cassettes	No	No	Yes	Yes	Yes	NA
Video discs	Yes[2]	No	Yes	Yes	Yes	NA
Teletext	No	Yes	No[3]	No	No	Yes
Videotext	Yes	Yes	Yes	No	No	Yes

NA Not applicable

[1]Some cable TV systems are being built with two-way capability, but are limited in comparison to the computer-based interaction of videotext.

[2]Optical type has random access capability allowing some interactive uses.

[3]Broadcast teletext restricted to the VBI has limited storage; cable teletext can use full channels and has greater storage.

Source: The author

York-based market research firm, is that, by 1990, cable advertising volume will approach $2.5 billion—or 20 to 25% of cable revenues.[1] To put things in perspective, however, that figure must be compared to projected 1990 advertising expenditures of the traditional media: $10 billion for magazines; $34.5 billion for television; $11.3 billion for radio; $46 billion for newspapers; and $20 billion for direct mail. Another study, by the editors of Knowledge Industry Publications, Inc., projected a slightly higher proportional advertising volume for cable of $2.7 billion by 1990. Figures for other media include $29.4 billion for television, $41 billion for newspapers, $8.3 billion for magazines and $9.9 billion for radio.[2]

The major advertising advantage of cable TV is that it can use full video, including color, motion and sound. It can provide "live" explanations or demonstrations of goods and services, as is done by the shopping shows described in Chapter 4. A promising variation of this approach is the use of cable TV for delivering "on-demand" video. For advertising applications, the first example of this is the "Cableshop" service, which

---

[1]Link Resources Corporation, "Emerging Advertising Forms in the New Electronic Media " (New York, November 1981).

[2]Knowledge Industry Publications, Inc., *The Cable Television Advertising Market 1982-87* (White Plains, NY, 1982), p. 79.

allows viewers to call up specific advertisements. This service is also described in Chapter 4. Of course, cable can also carry traditional television advertising.

One of the most exciting possibilities for cable TV is to combine it with other technologies. As mentioned previously, cable TV is still limited by a lack of reliable methods for measuring audiences, and its advertising effectiveness and efficiency are in question. Methods other than standard audience measurement techniques are being developed to track consumer behavior after exposure to specific commercials. Two research companies in particular, Information Resources, Inc. and Selling Areas Marketing, Inc. (SAMI), have worked to combine cable TV with electronic product scanners at supermarket checkouts. Ads are transmitted by cable TV to participating homes. Later purchases by consumers from those homes can be recorded using the scanners and magnetic identification cards. By correlating this data with the commercials to which the consumers have been exposed, these firms hope to rate the effectiveness of individual advertising campaigns.

VIDEO CASSETTES

Video cassettes, like cable TV, have been considered for advertising use because of the upsurge of interest in cassettes for entertainment. Advertising could lower the high prices consumers now must pay for video cassettes. However, viewers' ability to "fast-forward" and avoid commercials altogether simply by pushing a button on their video cassette players limits the appeal of this use. A more likely possibility would be the development of video cassettes with promotional, instructional or informational content closely tied to a specific sponsor, as discussed in Chapter 1.

OPTICAL VIDEO DISCS

Video discs have received more attention than video cassettes as an advertising medium. Most interesting are the mass storage and interactive capabilities of the video disc. A single video disc can be used to store 54,000 frames of information per side. Each frame can be a still photograph (pictures, words or both) or one of a series of moving frames. Because optical video discs can allow random access to any individual frame within a few seconds, interactive catalogs have been widely discussed as an application.

The first advertiser to try using the video disc was Sears, which put a 236-page catalog on a disc during 1981 and conducted a trial in a limited number of its catalog showrooms and with 1000 households owning video disc players. Sears blended still frames with moving sequences, providing

17 merchandise sections on the disc. Using an index, consumers could find specific merchandise and then see a demonstration. Altogether 18,000 products were shown on the disc. If played straight through, the disc would have run for 28 minutes, but it was designed to be browsed in a random fashion similar to a printed catalog. Sears has released few of its findings about the effectiveness of the video disc, except that women were less willing than men to operate the video disc during the test.

Video discs have serious shortcomings as a medium for catalogs, however. Companies such as Sears, which spent $100 million on printed catalogs in 1980, have considered video discs as one way to beat the high costs of printing and mailing catalogs. But although video discs can store a large catalog's worth of information—more than many of today's specialized catalogs even need—they cannot be updated. New discs would have to be "printed" as often as are traditional print catalogs. In addition, the consumer market for disc players has been slow to materialize. Although the optical video disc was first introduced in 1978 by Magnavox Company, fewer than 100,000 players are now in the field, and DiscoVision Associates, one of the major disc manufacturers, closed one of its two operations in early 1982. Optical players remain very expensive, and the number of people who could use a video disc catalog at home is very small. A more appropriate setting might be in stores or catalog showrooms.

The video disc has also been suggested as a mate for videotext, providing a video component in a larger home information system, but again, the sheer cost of the hardware bars such a dual-technology system for the foreseeable future.

TELETEXT

Teletext—one-way information retrieval systems carried by broadcast or cable—is being explored for its advertising potential. System operators, such as Keycom Electronic Publishing and Time Video Information Services, are struggling with several issues, including pricing and the possibility of revenue loss from normal TV advertising. A recent study of the advertising revenue potential of electronic publishing systems, including teletext and videotext, concluded that the potential is "substantial" and that, in fact, electronic publishing services must tap advertising revenues if they are to succeed on a large scale.[3]

---

[3]Communications Studies and Planning International, Inc., "The Advertising Value of Electronic Publishing Systems," (New York, November 1982).

Teletext is more like visual radio or a video newspaper than it is like TV. People are likely to turn to it for brief periods and for specific needs such as headline news, sports results, weather reports, travel schedules, entertainment listings or to play the occasional game. Advertising such as classifieds and infomercials incorporated with this type of information could become very appealing to advertisers when research becomes reliable enough to validate such viewing. In Great Britain, where commercial teletext is available and 750,000 teletext-equipped TV sets were in place by the end of 1982, teletext advertising has already made its initial appearance on the two commercial broadcast services.

VIDEOTEXT

The significance of videotext, both for advertisers and consumers, is that it is two-way and incorporates the power of the computer. While videotext is still in the trial stage—not yet successfully demonstrated as an effective promotional vehicle—it will emerge over this decade as the most powerful of all the new electronic media for transactions. Videotext provides the user with unique "on-demand" video capability to access large amounts of information and to take immediate follow-up action. No other medium can make this claim.

Advantages and Disadvantages of Advertising on Videotext

Although experience with videotext advertising is still limited, several interesting points have emerged.

- Unlike print ads, videotext advertising can seldom be based on a single frame, but requires a series of frames.

- Videotext has no discrete physical package, but exists as a data base in which users can look up specific pages of information on demand.

- Indexing and cross-referencing are key attributes.

- Graphics are, and will probably remain, inferior to print and video graphics.

- Videotext is unobtrusive and requires outside advertising—in print and broadcast—to spur users into action, as for example in the Cox Index system, in which advertisers can present their information

Hombanc is part of the package of information and transactional services co-ordinated by HomServ as part of the Cox Index system in Omaha, NE. The keypad allows the customer to conduct two-way transactions with a bank, for example, to pay bills. Courtesy HomServ, Inc.

both on a continuous full video channel and as a series of videotext frames; viewers using the system can switch back and forth between the two.

In addition to these more or less physical attributes, more abstract characteristics will affect the use of videotext. Unlike most other media, videotext is relatively blind to "straight" versus promotional information. Indeed, videotext tends to blur the differences between the two. For example, if a drug company provides suggestions on better living, these would be considered an advertisement—and easily recognizable as such—in most conventional media. In videotext, because of limitations in frame size and graphics, such an ad is difficult to distinguish from other frames of information. This raises questions about regulation of advertising.

In England, British Telecom (BT), which operates the Prestel system, has tried to steer clear of controversies surrounding content or charges of government censorship by stressing its role as a common carrier. Contracts with information providers require them to indemnify BT against legal actions resulting from material carried by Prestel. Except in clear cases of "bad taste," BT maintains its arms-length relationship to content. Meanwhile, the Association of Viewdata Information Providers, a British trade group, has adopted a code of ethics that covers advertising. However, most of the document is derived from regulations for conventional forms of advertising, emphasizing the usual prohibitions against misleading claims, immorality, etc. In only a few stipulations does it really take note of videotext's characteristics. For example, it requires that advertisers indicate within their frames that their message is an advertisement.

In the U.S., there has been discussion of possible federal regulation of advertising. In such a case, the watchdog role could fall to several agencies. The Federal Trade Commission (FTC) traditionally has played the largest role in regulating advertising. One of its major activities has been to require that certain advertisements it judged incomplete or misleading be amended with disclaimers or other notes. Such a requirement might limit the appeal of videotext for advertisers due to the constricted format of the video display. Most videotext systems can accommodate a maximum of 960 characters per screen, though very few actually use even half this many. A disclaimer might well occupy more than half a videotext frame. Also, since videotext does not offer the range of type sizes available in print, disclaimers would be in letters of about the same size as the advertisement itself.

However, in an era that favors "unleashing" market forces, it seems unlikely that the government will be quick to tackle the thorny issues of regulating electronic publishing unless it is forced to do so. Despite many attempts, Congress has yet to pass a new telecommunications bill to replace the Communications Act of 1934. And there are good arguments against regulation of content of U.S. videotext. Richard M. Neustadt, in *The Birth of Electronic Publishing,* mentions the following:

- Electronic publishing is an abundant, almost unlimited market, not a scarce public resource (the legal basis for regulating content of broadcasts).

- Videotext is not pervasive; information is called up by choice.

- Overregulation might strangle the emerging medium.[4]

Apart from these concerns, videotext must still define its niche within the existing media mix. To gain acceptance a new medium usually must identify itself as a "new, improved" version of something already established. Then gradually it begins to find its unique role. In terms of advertising, videotext has only begun to evolve. Therefore it is appropriate to examine videotext in terms of existing forms of advertising that it can provide—classifieds (including electronic Yellow Pages) and display advertising.

Classified Advertising and Electronic Yellow Pages

The best evidence of videotext's potential power as a classified advertising vehicle comes from the newspaper industry. Newspapers have climbed on the videotext bandwagon as a defensive maneuver to protect against loss of a valuable source of revenue, classified advertising. In 1981, newspaper advertising revenues were $17.6 billion, of which $14.7 billion was local advertising. Classifieds accounted for $4.7 billion of the local advertising.[5] The newspaper industry's motto about videotext might be: "If you can't beat it, use it." In the U.S., no fewer than 15 newspapers have launched videotext activities, at a cost estimated in 1981 by Link to have been about $15 million.[6]

Several characteristics of videotext make it ideal for classified advertising. Videotext can distribute advertisements to any videotext user, regard-

---

[4]Richard M. Neustadt, *The Birth of Electronic Publishing: Legal and Economic Issues in Telephone, Cable and Over-the-Air Teletext and Videotext* (White Plains, NY: Knowledge Industry Publications, Inc., 1982), pp. 38-41.

[5]American Newspaper Publishers Association, *Facts about Newspapers* (April 1982).

[6]Link Resources Corp., "Emerging Advertising Forms."

less of whether he lives within the geographical confines of the newspaper's traditional reach. All classified listings can be updated immediately, thus sparing both buyer and seller the needless searching of out-of-date and inappropriate offers. All listings can be indexed and cross-referenced in ways that would be impractical for printed material or even teletext. Today's print classifieds must be divided into categories that make the most sense to the largest number of people. With videotext, the classifieds data base could be searched by each individual according to his own criteria. By using several keywords, the user could let the computer select only advertisements appropriate to his needs, rather than scanning long columns of print. Cross-referencing capabilities would link classified announcements to other parts of the data base. For example, vacation homes for rent could be cross-referenced to travel information, airline schedules, local event guides, currency exchange rates, etc. Finally, videotext's two-way communications capability could allow immediate responses.

Unlike many of the other applications being proposed or developed at present, classified advertising offers obvious benefits for its users. Potential savings in time and money with electronic classifieds are indisputable. Furthermore, electronic classifieds are not susceptible to the problems that many other videotext applications have because the medium is "unobtrusive." Users of classifieds are actively looking for information and do not require prompting. Moreover, classifieds do not rely on graphics—the Achilles heel of videotext. Finally, both telephone companies and newspapers are already set up to sell, accept and organize electronic classified advertising. Years of experience—and investments already made in electronic editing equipment—should pay off in the videotext arena.

CompuServe has already initiated a national classified service in a trial with the Newspaper Advertising Bureau, which supplies information from 11 participating newspapers. Subscribers to CompuServe can access information on job listings, vacation homes, classic cars and the like.

Newspapers have not been alone in their interest in using videotext for classified advertising. Telephone companies, both in the U.S. and abroad, have competed with them for this franchise. "Electronic Yellow Pages" have become a controversial area of the new electronic media, throwing into question the ability of some forms of print publishing to survive against the onslaught of computers and telecommunications. Telephone companies have argued that "going electronic" with their publications is their birthright in an electronic world—in effect, an extension of their multibillion-dollar-a-year Yellow Pages publishing business.[7] But the ability of

---

[7] AT&T's directory revenues in 1981 were estimated at $2.45 billion with pre-tax earnings of 12%. James A. White, "Yellow Pages Turning Gold for Publishers," *Wall Street Journal* (November 16, 1981).

electronic Yellow Pages to be updated any time sets a clear course of conflict with newspapers' classified advertisements.

Before the AT&T settlement, newspaper publishers were strongly challenging the right of telecommunications companies to enter the business of providing information electronically when they already controlled the communication lines to distribute that information. During 1981, a group of publishers, led by the American Newspaper Publishers Association, successfully defeated a planned trial by AT&T to test an electronic Yellow Pages system in Austin, TX. Among the newspapers' concerns was AT&T's plan to offer "sales/special ads designed to provide supermarkets, department stores, and other businesses with a vehicle to highlight merchandise on a frequently changing basis." In AT&T's words, this service would have allowed retailers to "build an electronic catalog."[8]

The publishers and AT&T began to skirmish in a district court in Texas. Eventually, citing "protracted regulatory and legal proceedings," AT&T cancelled its plans—for the moment. Just six months later, the landmark AT&T settlement erased any question that it was legal for telephone companies, at least at the local level, to compete with publishers in originating information and advertising, as well as in transmitting it. However, one of the many unanswered questions of the settlement is whether AT&T will be able to compete in a full publishing capacity.

In Canada, where these legal and regulatory questions have not cropped up, Bell Canada has been publishing electronic Yellow Pages. Through its subsidiary Tele-Direct Publications, which publishes telephone directories, Bell Canada has created a data base of 7000 listings and advertisements taken from the Toronto and Quebec City print directories. This electronic data base is being used in Project Vista, a Bell Canada videotext trial that began in 1981.

In Europe, legal questions have been raised similar to those in the U.S. Early in 1983, the French national telephone company, the Ministry of Post, Telecommunications and Television (PTT), announced the official inauguration of its plan to replace printed telephone directories with videotext terminals in homes and offices. While many observers have hailed the French project as a brilliant means of overcoming the escalating costs of printing and distributing telephone books, publishers have been less enthusiastic. They claim that the national telephone monopoly is a direct, unfair threat to their survival. At issue is not the PTT's right to offer electronic Yellow Pages, but its right to update the listings anytime, the

---

[8]Statements quoted in Link Resources Corp., "Emerging Advertising Forms."

same criticism that was being leveled at AT&T.

While newspapers and telecommunications companies usually have been characterized as foes, there have been a number of attempts at cooperation. The most notable was the 1981 Viewtron test, a joint venture of AT&T and the Knight-Ridder subsidiary, Viewdata Corp. of America. As was described in Chapter 5, these two organizations have continued their cooperation and plan a larger test for 1983. General Telephone & Electronics Corporation (GTE) proposed during 1980-1981 to tie local newspapers together into a national videotext network, in which advertising revenue would be split between local newspapers, acting as sales agents and GTE, acting as the system operator. For a number of reasons, however, this proposal was never carried out.

Another example of cooperation involves CompuServe and several newspapers. Initially the service ran daily editorial material from such papers as *The New York Times, The Los Angeles Times, The Washington Post* and others. This was scheduled to be supplemented with the papers' classified advertising during 1982. This relationship, however, has not been without its problems. One controversy came from an unexpected source: Comp-U-Card, the electronic shopping service also carried by CompuServe (see Chapter 5). At the time that CompuServe began working with Comp-U-Card (an independent company), a number of the newspapers protested that Comp-U-Card competed with the local retailers who place ads in their papers. The issue has not been resolved. The service has been curtailed, with only *The Washington Post,* Canadian Press and one local newspaper remaining.

In many cases, newspapers have responded to the competitive challenge of telecommunications firms by themselves entering the business of both producing and distributing information electronically. Dow Jones, publisher of *The Wall Street Journal* and a number of other publications, has become both an information provider and a system operator. It plans to exploit its satellite network—today used only for transmitting its editions to regional printing plants—to deliver national information to local videotext systems. Unlike Dow Jones, most newspapers in the U.S. are local, not national. Consequently, many have established themselves as videotext systems operators in their traditional franchise areas. Included in this group are *The Chicago Sun-Times, The Fort Worth Star-Telegram, The Los Angeles Times, The Boston Globe* and *The Dallas Morning News.*

The decision of many publishers to enter the videotext business quickly has also been driven by fears of action by local cable TV operators, who have shown increasing interest in interactive services both as a revenue-producing activity and as a sign of their commitment to providing community services demanded by local pressure. Newspaper publishers have long been ambivalent toward cable TV. Many newspaper companies also own cable TV systems, although cross-ownership rules prohibit newspapers from controlling cable TV systems in the same service area.

A number of newspapers have leased channels on local cable systems, giving them an additional "access vehicle" to reach their markets. Throughout the 1970s, the availability of inexpensive channels (sometimes altogether free) enabled newspapers to experiment with cable advertising, with little concern for quality or success. By 1980, however, newspapers began to find cable channels no longer available at cheap rates. As a result, they began to reassess their half-hearted approach to the medium, and began to develop higher quality electronic programs. Two newspapers in particular, *The St. Louis Post-Dispatch* and *The Fort Worth Star-Telegram,* have developed packages geared to local markets, combining news, features and advertising.

The participation of newspapers is a positive factor for the development of electronic marketing. Newspapers have traditionally been strong marketers within their communities and can bring buyers and sellers together in a cost-effective manner that no other medium can duplicate.

Display Advertising

Display advertising presents opportunities and obstacles quite different from those for classified advertising. Display advertisements—in newspapers, magazines and catalogs—have evolved toward ever-better graphics. The use of color art and full color photographs has become increasingly important. Most merchandisers agree that better artwork sells more goods.

Entering this scene, videotext is immediately faced with the problem of its graphics, which are poor by the standards of display advertising. Videotext can display static pages of information in a variety of colors using relatively simple graphics. Photographs have been transmitted in experimental systems, but will not be a part of videotext until the 1990s, if at all. Aside from the difficulties of transmitting the photographs themselves is the problem of TV set resolution (the degree to which a system can record fine detail), which is currently relatively poor, especially on U.S. TV sets.

In part because of an aggressive campaign waged by British, French and Canadian videotext promoters against each other, the issue of graphics has persisted. While the British were the first into the marketplace with their videotext technology, their graphic capabilities were inferior to the French

The Viewmart directory offers consumers a "video shopping center." The display is made appealing through the use of color and videotext graphics. Courtesy ViewMart, Inc.

technology introduced soon after. The Canadians, however, claimed their Telidon system was a breakthrough because of its alphageometric graphics, which gave a higher resolution image, as illustrated in Chapter 5. A number of potential system operators pledged their loyalty to Telidon on the basis of its superior graphics. However, advertisers have been "underwhelmed" by even the Telidon graphics.

Despite the limitations of videotext, a number of advertisers have attempted instant specials, mini-catalogs and extra product information supplements. In Britain, advertisers on Prestel have included department stores, mail-order companies, travel companies and publishers. During the Viewtron test in Coral Gables, FL (see Chapter 5) about a dozen advertisers promoted wares ranging from food to marine supplies to books. Overall, however, advertisers have had difficulty in developing new creative techniques for the medium, choosing to apply conventional print techniques to the electronic screen. Because of the small number of videotext users, advertisers have not been able to measure the effectiveness of specific electronic advertising techniques.

CONCLUSION

Although a wide variety of new delivery systems is becoming available for advertising, only a tiny fraction of media budgets has been diverted from traditional advertising outlets such as radio, television, newspaper and magazines. Cable TV has fared best, but it managed to attract less than $200 million in advertising revenues in 1982, and most of those expenditures were for 30-second spot ads identical to those run on broadcast television. Advertising using other new media systems seems more exotic than practical at the present time, despite a good deal of discussion.

Nevertheless, over the longer term, advertising will find its place in these new media. Cable is expected to become a favored medium for direct marketers once they discover that it more resembles radio and magazines than television in its delivery and distribution patterns to consumers. Videotext could be the real sleeper in advertising. Eventually, electronic Yellow Pages and classified advertising will become the saviors of videotext. AT&T is eagerly eying the electronic Yellow Pages market and trying to position itself so that it can deliver this service despite the entreaties of competitors opposing such a move. The same holds true for the newspaper industry, which will zealously protect its classified ad franchise from the encroachment of competitors who would like to gain a slice of this business by exploiting electronic delivery.

Electronic marketing will have to rely on large-scale advertising support to finance its development and growth. Subscriber and transaction fees for services will not be sufficient to support widespread use. The real breakthrough will probably not take place until the late 1980s, when the various players will have a better idea of what services they can deliver profitably to substantial numbers of viewers.

7

The Future of Electronic Marketing

The concept of electronic marketing is not necessarily new. It goes back to the early days of radio when advertisers discovered, to their delight, that the medium could be used to sell their products. Over the years, the techniques of electronic marketing have been expanded and refined. Recently, the telephone has been combined with television to produce direct response advertising, first on commercial television and now on cable.

Electronic transactions on the new electronic media are more akin to direct marketing than to traditional retailing. Like direct marketing, electronic marketing provides consumers the opportunity to shop for goods and services without visiting offices or retail stores. Transactions are conducted through communication links and electronic images rather than with salespeople and merchandise displays. Both direct and electronic marketing combine an offer of goods or services with advertising, and both give the seller a way to measure precisely the offer's success. Direct marketing, which has been growing vigorously despite the recessionary economy (by most estimates it is growing twice as fast as retailing), is expected to be a primary beneficiary of the new electronic technologies.

HOW ELECTRONIC MARKETING WILL EVOLVE

The use of cable for electronic marketing should continue to increase significantly. The current cable shopping channels, which are basically extensions of traditional advertising and selling methods using television, will probably not survive their beleaguered status since they fail to attract enough viewers to make them paying propositions. However, in the long run cable will be used much more creatively for catalog selling using direct marketing techniques developed for two-way systems. When cable systems are equipped with addressable converters that can send signals on a selective basis to individual subscribers, advertising can be targeted geographically, demographically and psychographically, much like direct mail offers.

The new videotext, teletext and home computer technologies have the potential to make electronic marketing more interactive than ever before —but in order for this to happen, advertisers will need a mass audience of millions of individuals operating from remote terminals. To attract such substantial audiences, text and graphic video services will have to borrow heavily from classified advertising and electronic Yellow Pages directories. These applications will be more immediately perceived as useful than video catalogs or video display ads directed to subscribers who are used to print versions. Moreover, systems will evolve that combine full cable channels with text and graphic offerings where users will be able to switch back and forth as required. Such a system is already available in Great Britain; viewers on the commercial channels are given cues to switch to a specific page on the teletext service for more detailed information on an offer.

Traditional broadcast commercials that blanket an entire market will not disappear, but their use will be questioned and their effectiveness will decline as consumers look to cable, videotext, video discs and even print for information content. Traditional advertising on broadcast television will be used increasingly for image building and consumer awareness but can be expected to adopt more of the characteristics of direct response ads as sponsors demand greater accountability for their media expenditures.

Videotext and teletext will provide enormous amounts of consumer feedback, which will be part of the two-way connection established by the new forms of electronic marketing. Market research, product development, product management, advertising and distribution will be affected as data on consumer responses are fed to computers for continuous analysis and interpretation.

Obstacles to the Development of Electronic Marketing

It would be a mistake, however, to suggest that information age marketing procedures will simply evolve. Trials of many types of hardware, software and communication systems will continue over the next few years to test factors ranging from technical features to consumer demand. At present, leading banks and publishers seem to be the most interested in testing and development.

One important issue is the role that AT&T will be allowed to play in the home services field. This question is complicated further by the reorganization of the giant utility as ordered by the January 1982 Justice Department antitrust settlement. The settlement bars AT&T from providing electronic services on its own facilities until 1991, after which one must assume it will be allowed to conduct this activity. However, what is not clear is whether AT&T could provide services such as its Yellow Pages through the facilities of third party organizations such as divested Bell operating companies or independent telephone companies. In fact, AT&T officials have already hinted that this course of action is under consideration. If AT&T is allowed an active role in electronic publishing, the roles of broadcasters, newspapers and cable in providing services to the home market will be seriously diminished. Opposition by AT&T's competitors is almost certain.

Beyond the uncertainty that the AT&T issue raises, there are other obstacles to the full-scale application of new electronic technologies to marketing and distribution. First, the systems themselves are enormously expensive to develop. Participants will have to consider joint ventures to offset their own weaknesses in one or more areas and to gain capital.

Second, there are problems for consumers, which could affect their acceptance of new technologies for marketing. At first, it was assumed that "fear of technology" would be a restrictive factor in attracting the mass market. Sales of personal computers, the phenomenal success of video games and the penetration of VCRs and pay TV are all indications that consumers are more than willing to confront the new electronic media. Much of this success, however, is entertainment driven; consumers appear quite willing to spend their time and money to be amused.

Success will not come as easily for non-entertainment applications. The cost of the hardware and software for establishing and using home services could be a real problem in moving the market beyond the early adopter level. Personal computers, decoders, videotext terminals and modems are all part of the hardware package required to access the new technology. The package can run anywhere from $500 to $2000 per household at today's prices. Volume production is needed to bring costs down but that is hard to achieve without an obvious market. In addition, subscriber fees, transaction fees and usage costs have to be paid. These costs may more than offset any possible savings that are attained by eliminating a certain amount of "traditional" shopping. And it is questionable whether consumers will really be better informed to make purchasing decisions because they are interacting with computerized data bases.

Aside from dollar costs, the human aspects of getting people to use electronic services must be considered. A video screen (unless used for business) is perceived by consumers as a source of entertainment. Using it for shopping, banking or sending messages to friends and neighbors is a somewhat alien concept. Furthermore, a computer package is not portable, it is hard to browse through an electronic data base, the displays don't show what a product really looks like and there is limited space for textual material. (See Figure 7.1 for a sample transaction.)

Finally, there are problems of security and privacy. Home banking offers an example. One of the big problems in developing home banking is customer concern about someone gaining unauthorized access to an account, and elaborate safeguards are being built into the system to prevent such an occurrence. The widespread acceptance of automatic teller machines, however, would seem to indicate that customer fears about using automated procedures for personal banking can be overcome once a sufficient level of confidence in the systems is reached.

Electronic marketing, using two-way systems, also has the capability to collect vast amounts of information on the consumer's "buying profile," which can be stored in the data bases of network operators, service providers and information providers. The possibility of unauthorized diversion of such information to third parties causes concern among consumers.

THE FUTURE OF ELECTRONIC MARKETING

All these questions can only be raised at this time, not answered. But answers must be found soon if electronic marketing is to begin moving toward its potential. An increasingly "computer literate" consumer has demonstrated an interest in the new technology and has enthusiastically embraced certain forms of entertainment and personal computing capability. This will be an important factor in the support of non-entertainment services such as electronic marketing, but it does not mean that the trend is strong enough yet to ensure success. Consumer demand for these services is uncertain, to say the least.

The Role of the Business Sector

The strongest push will come not from consumers but rather from the business organizations anxious to contain costs, enter new markets, offer better customer service or to stave off competition. As we have seen, those taking the lead are banks, publishers and, to a lesser extent, broadcasters, with the cable and telecommunications people waiting for the opportune moment.

The development of services aimed squarely at consumers could be premature at this time—unless a long-term payout of at least 5 to 10 years is acceptable. The tests described in Chapters 4 and 5, conducted by Knight-Ridder, Times Mirror Cable, Time, Cox Index and CBS, all offer consumer-oriented services. Since all of these organizations serve consumer markets as their primary business, it stands to reason that their entry into

Figure 7.1: A Sample Transaction on Comp-U-Store
Subscriber responses are printed in bold face.

!!!! HOWDY SHOPPER !!!!

Enter:
  (1) HELP & Information
  (2) Shopping & Ordering
  (3) Databasement (bargains)
2
Enter: Product
TV
Enter: Brand name
  (NP) No preference
RCA
Color or black & white
  (1) Color
  (2) Black & white
1
Screen size
  (NP) No preference
  (1) 12 or 13 inches
  (2) 14 or 15 inches
  (3) 17 or 18 inches
  (4) 19 inches
4
Ship to State (necessary for quote)
CT
Ship to Zip Code (necessary for quote)
06477
What's the most you will spend?
$500
Television

#	MFG	Model	FDC
1	RCA	FRG475W	331.89
2	RCA	FGR440S	333.62

Enter: an item # or (CHA) to change
2
    Television
Mfg: RCA   Model FGR440S
    Description
19″ color portable TV with pushbutton tuning.
Features room light sensor and sharpness
control. Silver finished cabinet.
Want to order? (Y or N)
Y
May I have your credit card number, please.

———

Source: Adapted from a Comp-U-Store printout; courtesy Comp-U-Card of
America, Inc. Used with permission.

electronic publishing and marketing would also be directed at consumers.

However, before electronic marketing and other services reach the consumer market on a commercially viable basis, an incubation period in the business sector may be required. It is in this area that videotext, video discs, cable and even teletext could be developed. Private videotext or "closed user group" systems would be attractive to business executives, professionals, engineers, travel agents, real estate brokers and entertainment organizations. Many of these groups are already served by extensive online systems. With the proliferation of personal computers, there will be a growing demand for simplified online systems that can be accessed from practically any desk-top terminal. When the "average" American executive or professional is willing to work from his own terminal, the prospects for private videotext will rise immeasurably. The use of computers by executives in Japan is already widespread. In the U.S. however, executives have yet to overcome not only a resistance to computers but also the notion that anything with a keyboard is for clerical workers.

Videotext, teletext and video discs installed in public locations could also be used by consumers on a self-service basis. Travel agencies, real estate firms, stock brokerage offices, banks and some retailers could use these media to provide information, to demonstrate products and to conduct transactions. This could all be done on an unaided or aided basis depending upon the location, the consumer, the type of information and the possible transactions. Business rather than consumers would support these systems financially. Advertising revenue could also be expected.

The availability of such systems at the business level would not only aid the organizations who supported them, but it would also begin sensitizing the mass market for extension of the same services into the home. It is an intermediate step, but it may be a necessary one if the objectives of the new electronic media in developing the home market are to be met.

The Impact of Electronic Marketing

Retail stores will not disappear soon, but sellers are expected to make increasing use of technology. Over the longer term, the strategies of banks, retailers and service organizations will have to change. Retail space will be planned and used differently; banks will emphasize electronic branches rather than brick and mortar ones; retail travel agencies will go "electronic," closing many of their storefront locations; real estate brokers will do the same by providing electronic listings and floor plans to interested buyers. In real estate transactions, brokers, buyers and sellers will be able to "meet" electronically, without any geographic restrictions.

In time, airlines, hotels and real estate owners may offer direct connections to consumers, as may some manufacturers who now sell products through dealers. Many possibilities are appearing in a world where communications, computers and television will be combined to transform traditional sales and distribution patterns.

By the early 1990s, full-scale electronic transaction, information and communication systems will emerge to serve the needs of consumers. They will be run by well-heeled organizations who will package both information and services and who will be capable of managing all the components, including communications, data processing, marketing and customer service. In a sense, these organizations will be highly diversified utilities, offering a package of services to subscribers, who will pay an annual membership fee in addition to usage charges.

These one-stop shopping systems will offer everything from apples to zippers as well as a full range of services: banking, investments, insurance, travel and real estate. Educational programs and electronic mail will also be included. The subscriber will have a choice of systems, at international, national or regional levels.

Establishing organizations of this type will require enormous capital and cooperation between participants. The impact of the changes that result will also raise many new issues. Responsibilities to consumers will include not only guarantees of privacy and security but also customer service and protection against fraudulent claims and deceptive advertising. Who should be responsible—the information provider or the system operator? What information will be allowed and what will be barred? More important, who will decide? And in a society where electronic access becomes increasingly important, what rights will the economically disadvantaged have? The danger of even wider divisions between economic classes is quite evident.

It's understandable if the developments described in this book seem somewhat fanciful. For too long, we have been prisoners of a system that is rooted in the nineteenth century. Although television has transformed the world in the delivery of news and entertainment, it has done little to ease the shopper's burden or to offer a wider range of choices for goods and services that must be purchased regularly. The information age is making advanced electronic marketing possible and can greatly increase the options we have for selling and buying. It's not a question of "if" but "when."

Appendix: Organizations Involved with Electronic Marketing

ADAMS-RUSSELL CO., INC.
1380 Main St.
Waltham, MA 02154

**AFFILIATED PUBLICA-
TIONS, INC.**
135 Morrissey Blvd.
Boston, MA 02107

**AMERICAN BROADCASTING
CO., INC. (ABC)**
1330 Ave. of the Americas
New York, NY 10019

AMERICAN EXPRESS CO.
American Express Plaza
New York, NY 10004

**AMERICAN TELEPHONE
AND TELEGRAPH (AT&T)**
195 Broadway
New York, NY 10007

**AMERICAN TELEVISION
AND COMMUNICATIONS
CORP. (ATC)**
160 Inverness Dr. W.
Englewood, CO 80112

**AMERICAN VIDEO
SHOPPER**
2401 21st Ave. S.
Nashville, TN 37212

APPLE COMPUTER, INC.
10260 Bandley Dr.
Cupertino, CA 95014

ASSOCIATED PRESS
50 Rockefeller Plaza
New York, NY 10020

ATARI, INC.
1265 Borregas Ave.
Sunnyvale, CA 94086

**AUTOMATIC DATA PRO-
CESSING, INC. (ADP)**
405 Route 3
Clifton, NJ 07015

BANK OF AMERICA NT&SA
Bank of America Ctr.
P.O. Box 37000
San Francisco, CA 94137

BELL CANADA
25 Eddy St.
Hull, Quebec, Canada J8Y6N4

BILDSCHIRMTEXT
Deutsche Bundespost
Postfach 80 01
5300 Bonn 1, West Germany

BRITISH BROADCASTING CORPORATION (BBC)
Broadcasting House
London W1A 1AA, England

BRITISH TELECOM
OLC 3.1
55 Old Broad St.
London EC2M 1RX, England

CABLE NEWS NETWORK (CNN)
1050 Techwood Dr., NW
Atlanta, GA 30318

CABLEVISION SYSTEM DEVELOPMENT CORP.
1 Media Crossways
Woodbury, NY 11797

CAPITAL CITIES COMMUNICATIONS
485 Madison Ave.
New York, NY 10022

CBS, INC.
51 W. 52 St.
New York, NY 10022

CENTRAL TELEPHONE AND UTILITIES CORP. (CENTEL)
O'Hare Plaza
5725 N.E. River Rd.
Chicago, IL 60631

CHASE MANHATTAN BANK
1 Chase Manhattan Plaza
New York, NY 10081

CHEMICAL BANK
20 Pine St.
New York, NY 10005

CHRISTIAN BROADCAST NETWORK (CBN)
CBN Ctr.
Virginia Beach, VA 23463

CITIBANK
399 Park Ave.
New York, NY 10043

COMMODORE INTERNATIONAL LTD.
950 Rittenhouse Rd.
Norristown, PA 19403

COMP-U-CARD OF AMERICA, INC.
777 Summer St.
Stamford, CT 06901

COMPUSERVE, INC.
5000 Arlington Centre Blvd.
Columbus, OH 43220

COX CABLE COMMUNICA-TIONS INC.
219 Perimeter Ctr Pkwy.
Atlanta, GA 30346

DIGITAL EQUIPMENT CORP.
129 Parker St.
Maynard, MA 01754

DOW JONES & CO., INC.
22 Cortlandt St.
New York, NY 10007

ENTERTAINMENT AND SPORTS PROGRAMMING NETWORK (ESPN)
ESPN Plaza
Bristol, CT 06010

FIELD ENTERPRISES
401 N. Wabash Ave.
Chicago, IL 60611

**FINANCIAL INTERSTATE
SERVICES CORP.**
P.O. Box 15003
Knoxville, TN 37901

FIRST BANK SYSTEMS, INC.
P.O. Box 422
Minneapolis, MN 55480

**GENERAL TELEPHONE &
ELECTRONICS CORP.
(GTE)**
1 Stamford Forum
Stamford, CT 06904

**GTE TELENET COMMUNI-
CATIONS CORP.**
8330 Old Courthouse Rd.
Vienna, VA 22180

HOMSERV, INC.
656 West Putnam
Greenwich, CT 06830

HONEYWELL, INC.
200 Smith St.
Waltham, MA 02154

**HUNTINGTON NATIONAL
BANK**
Huntington National Bank Bldg.
17 S. High St.
Columbus, OH 43260

IBM CORP.
Armonk, NY 10504

**INDEPENDENT BROAD-
CASTING AUTHORITY
(IBA)**
70 Brompton Rd.
London SW3 1EY, England

INFOMART, LTD.
164 Martin St.
Toronto, Ontario,
Canada M453A8

**INFORMATION RESOURCES,
INC.**
520 N. Dearborn Ave.
Chicago, IL 60610

INTELMATIQUE
98, Rue de Sevres
75007 Paris, France

KCET-TV
4400 Sunset Dr.
Los Angeles, CA 90027

**KEYCOM ELECTRONIC
PUBLISHING**
Schaumburg Corporate Center
1501 Woodfield Rd.
Suite 110 West
Schaumburg, IL 60195

**KNIGHT-RIDDER
NEWSPAPERS, INC.**
1 Herald Plaza
Miami, FL 33101

LEADER TELECABLE
611 S. Farwell
Eau Claire, WI 54701

MANHATTAN CABLE TV
120 E. 23 St.
New York, NY 10010

METROMEDIA
1 Harmon Plaza
Secaucus, NJ 07094

**MODERN SATELLITE
  NETWORK**
45 Rockefeller Plaza
New York, NY 10111

**NATIONAL BROADCASTING
  CO., INC. (NBC)**
30 Rockefeller Plaza
New York, NY 10020

NORPAK, LTD.
10 Hearst Way
Kanata, Ontario,
  Canada K2L2P4

OAK INDUSTRIES
16935 W. Bernardo Dr.
Rancho Bernardo, CA 92127

PRIME CABLE CORP.
1515 City National Bank Bldg.
Austin, TX 78701

RADIO SHACK
385 Fifth Ave.
New York, NY 10016

RCA CORP.
30 Rockefeller Plaza
New York, NY 10020

**SAMMONS
  COMMUNICATIONS**
P.O. Box 22578
Dallas, TX 75265

**SATELLITE PROGRAMMING
  NETWORK (SPN)**
P.O. Box 45684
Tulsa, OK 74145

**SATELLITE SYNDICATED
  SYSTEMS (SSS)**
8252 S. Harvard
Tulsa, OK 74136

SEARS, ROEBUCK & CO.
Sears Tower
Chicago, IL 60684

**SELLING AREAS
  MARKETING, INC.**
1271 Ave. of the Americas
New York, NY 10020

SHAWMUT BANK
1 Federal St.
Boston, MA 02211

SONY CORP. OF AMERICA
9 W. 57 St.
New York, NY 10019

**SOSKIN-THOMPSON
  ASSOCIATES**
655 Madison Ave.
New York, NY 10002

**SOURCE TELECOMPUTING
  CORP.**
1616 Anderson Rd.
McLean, VA 22102

SOUTHAM, INC.
321 Bloor E.
Toronto, Ontario, Canada

TAFT BROADCASTING
1718 Young St.
Cincinnati, OH 45210

TANDY CORP.
1600 One Tandy Ctr.
Fort Worth, TX 76102

**TELE-COMMUNICATIONS,
  INC.**
54 Denver Technological Ctr.
Denver, CO 80210

**TELEDIFFUSION DE
  FRANCE**
2127 Rue Barbes
Montrouge 92100, France

TELIDON CORP.
3 Landmark Sq.
Suite 400
Stamford, CT 06901

TEXAS INSTRUMENTS, INC.
P.O. Box 2474
Dallas, TX 75222

TICKETRON
1350 Ave. of the Americas
New York, NY 10019

TIME INC.
Time & Life Bldg.
New York, NY 10020

TIMES MIRROR CO.
Times Mirror Sq.
Los Angeles, CA 90053

TORSTAR CORP.
1 Yonge St.
Toronto, Ontario,
  Canada M5E1P9

TYMNET, INC.
20665 Valley Green Dr.
Cupertino, CA 95014

TYMSHARE, INC.
20705 Valley Green Dr.
Cupertino, CA 95014

**UNITED PRESS
  INTERNATIONAL**
220 E. 42 St.
New York, NY 10017

VIATEL CORP.
990 Washington St.
Dedham, MA 02026

VIDEOTEX AMERICA
1381 Morse Ave.
Irvine, CA 92714

**VIEWDATA CORP. OF
  AMERICA**
1111 Lincoln Rd.
Miami, FL 33139

VIEWMART, INC.
Suite 360
5620 Smetana Dr.
Minnetonka, MN 55343

**WARNER-AMEX CABLE
  COMMUNICATIONS**
75 Rockefeller Plaza
New York, NY 10019

**WARNER-AMEX SATELLITE
  ENTERTAINMENT CORP.**
1211 Ave. of the Americas
New York, NY 10036

**WATS MARKETING OF
    AMERICA**
3250 N. 93 St.
Omaha, NE 68134

WGBH-TV
125 Western Ave.
Boston, MA 02134

ZENITH CORP.
1000 N. Milwaukee Ave.
Glenview, IL 60025

Glossary

Alphageometric: Video display in which a microprocessor within the *terminal* "draws" the desired shape after beginning and end points have been transmitted with computer-coded picture description instructions (PDIs).

Alphamosaic: Video display in which each position on the screen consists of a grid of six squares, two across and three down, and the filling in of varying squares with light and dark shades to create a rough approximation of simple shapes.

Alphanumeric: Video display using text, numbers and primitive graphics.

Antiope: The French *teletext* system.

Basic cable: The services provided to a *cable television* system's subscribers for its minimum monthly fee.

Bildschirmtext: The German *videotext* system.

Cable shopping channel: A cable channel or program dedicated to product demonstrations using long-form commercials or *infomercials*.

Cable television: A communications system that transmits television signals by coaxial cable to subscriber sets.

Ceefax: The British Broadcasting Corporation (BBC) *teletext* system.

Character generator: An electronic device with a keyboard used to create *alphanumeric* displays on a video screen.

Decoder: An electronic device that translates signals transmitted in digital form back into the form of the original message.

Note: Words that appear in italics within definitions are defined elsewhere in this glossary.

Direct broadcast satellite (DBS): TV service that uses satellites to beam signals directly to small antennae installed by subscribers.

Direct marketing: Selling that uses one or more advertising media (e.g., direct mail, coupons, telephone, TV) to make a specific offer and elicit a response from the consumer.

Downstream: The direction from the *head-end* of a cable system to subscriber *terminals.*

Electronic funds transfer (EFT): A system that transfers money via telecommunications lines rather than by check or cash.

Electronic mail: A system of sending written messages over telephone lines, telex or computer data networks.

Electronic marketing: Selling, especially *direct marketing,* that uses computers, telecommunications and video display techniques rather than physical stores or print media to reach consumers.

Electronic newspaper: A news service transmitted electronically to remote *terminals.*

Fiber optics: A system that transmits voice, data and video by beaming light waves through very thin glass fibers.

Fragmentation: The splintering of mass TV audiences due to the proliferation of viewing choices.

Frame: The unit of *videotext* or *teletext* material that fills the screen when requested by the viewer; also referred to as a "screen" or "page."

Gateway: The capability to switch *videotext* users to outside or third-party data bases.

Head-end: The equipment that a cable system uses to distribute and receive subscriber signals and to receive externally transmitted signals from satellites or microwave transmitters.

High-definition television: An experimental TV system (already tested in Japan) that provides much clearer TV pictures with an increased number of scan lines and a wider viewing field; picture resolution is comparable to that of 35-mm film.

Infomercial: A hybrid sales message which combines editorial material with a sales message.

Infoserv provider: An organization that supplies information or services that can be accessed by *videotext* subscribers.

Interactive system: Generally refers to a *two-way cable* or telephone system capable of carrying information both from the *head-end* to the subscriber and from the subscriber back to the *head-end*.

Modem: For modulator/demodulator device, used to connect a *terminal* or home computer to a remote computer via telephone.

Multiple system operator (MSO): An organization that operates more than one *cable television* system.

Multi-point distribution system (MDS): A microwave transmission system used to send *pay TV* signals to subscribers with specially equipped TV sets.

Narrowcasting: Television programming designed for a specific audience.

New electronic media (NEM): A catch-all phrase used to describe delivery systems that offer alternatives to conventional television, such as cable, *pay TV,* video discs, video cassettes, *subscription TV,* etc.

Offline: In *electronic marketing,* refers to information or transactions not part of an information retrieval system on computer, cable, *videotext* or *teletext.*

Online: In *electronic marketing,* refers to information or transactions that are offered by an information retrieval system using computer, cable, *videotext* or *teletext.*

Oracle: The British commercial broadcast *teletext* system on Independent Television (ITV).

Page: See *frame.*

Pay cable: Programming distributed by cable for which subscribers pay a premium fee; used primarily to carry movies and sports.

Pay TV: Television for which the subscriber pays a fee (see *pay cable, subscription TV*).

Presentation level protocol (PLP): The videotext display standard announced by AT&T, which includes use of color and high quality graphics.

Prestel: British Telecom's two-way *videotext* system transmitted to subscribers by telephone.

Qube: The world's first commercial *two-way cable* system, operated by Warner Amex Cable.

Subscription television (STV): *Pay TV* transmitted by a broadcast station in coded form to subscribers with specially equipped TV sets.

Switching: The capability of a system to connect any two or more of its terminal points, such as the telephone system's ability to connect any two telephones.

System operator: An organization that manages a *videotext* system, usually a common carrier or a cable company.

Teletext: A one-way *videotext* service that transmits text and graphics images to specially equipped TV sets.

Telidon: The Canadian system of *teletext* and *videotext*.

Terminal: A device at an endpoint of a telecommunications channel that is capable of transmitting input and/or receiving output from a computer or *videotext* system.

Text and graphics TV: A television signal that provides *alphanumeric* and graphics displays; *videotext* and *teletext* fall into this category.

Tiered service: The offering of different packages of programs and services at varied prices on a cable TV system.

Time sharing: Multiple, simultaneous access of a remote computer by *terminals* from either the same or different organizations who need to use a common data base.

Two-way cable: An *interactive* cable system which allows the viewer to "talk back" to data bases connected to the system in order to shop, bank, retrieve information, cast a vote or communicate with other people on the network.

Upstream: The direction from the subscriber to the *head-end* of a cable system.

Vertical blanking interval (VBI): The unused lines in each frame of a television signal, which can be seen as a thick band when the TV picture rolls over; can be used for *teletext* or captioning.

Videotext: A term used to describe *text and graphics TV,* which can be either one- or two-way; sometimes reserved to describe a two-way system, as in this book; referred to as viewdata in Britain.

WATS: Acronym for Wide Area Telephone Service, which provides a dedicated line for incoming or outgoing calls for a flat monthly charge; incoming calls are toll-free to the originator.

Bibliography

SELECTED BOOKS, ARTICLES AND REPORTS

The Cable Television Advertising Market, 1982-87. White Plains, NY: Knowledge Industry Publications, Inc., 1982.

"Electronic Shopping Builds a Base." *Business Week,* October 26, 1981.

Fact Book on Direct Response Marketing. New York: Direct Marketing Association, Inc. Annual.

Floyd, Steve and Beth Floyd, eds., *Handbook of Interactive Video.* White Plains, NY: Knowledge Industry Publications, Inc., 1982.

"The Home Information Revolution." *Business Week,* June 29, 1981.

The Home Video and Cable Yearbook, 1982-1983. White Plains, NY: Knowledge Industry Publications, Inc., 1982.

Kaatz, Ronald B., *Cable: An Advertiser's Guide to the New Electronic Media.* Chicago: Crain Books, 1982.

McNair, Malcolm P. and Eleanor G. May, "The Next Revolution of the Retailing Wheel." *Harvard Business Review,* September-October 1978.

Rosenberg, Larry J. and Elizabeth C. Hirshman, "Retailing without Stores." *Harvard Business Review,* July-August 1980.

Sigel, Efrem *et al., The Future of Videotext: Worldwide Prospects for Home/Office Electronic Information Services.* White Plains, NY: Knowledge Industry Publications, Inc., 1983.

Sigel, Efrem *et al., Video Discs: The Technology, the Applications, and the Future.* White Plains, NY: Knowledge Industry Publications, Inc., 1980.

Stone, Bob, *Successful Direct Marketing Methods.* Chicago: Crain Books, 1979.

Strauss, Lawrence, *Home Video and Broadcasting: The Fight for Position, 1981-86.* White Plains, NY: Knowledge Industry Publications, Inc., 1981.

Tydeman, J. *et al., Teletext and Videotex in the United States; Market Potential, Technology, Public Policy Issues.* New York: McGraw-Hill Co., 1982.

Witek, John, *Response Television: Combat Advertising of the 1980s.* Chicago: Crain Books, 1981.

TRADE PUBLICATIONS

Advertising Age, Crain Communications, Inc., Chicago, IL (weekly).

Cablevision, Titsch Communications, Inc., Denver, CO (weekly).

Direct Marketing Magazine, Hoke Communications, Inc., Garden City, NY (monthly).

Electronic Media, Crain Communications, Inc., Chicago, IL (weekly).

Friday Report, Hoke Communications, Inc., Garden City, NY (weekly).

International Videotex Teletext News, Arlen Communications, Inc., Bethesda, MD (monthly).

Multichannel News, Fairchild Publications, Inc., Denver, CO (weekly).

Teleservices Report, Arlen Communications, Inc., Bethesda, MD (monthly).

Index

About the Author

Lawrence Strauss is a communications consultant whose activities have focused for the past six years on telecommunications and the new electronic media. During that period he has written four in-depth studies examining trends and applications of the new media as they relate to broadcasting, publishing, home video, cable TV, pay TV, teleshopping, advertising and home banking. He has consulted for such clients as GTE, AT&T, Western Electric, Northern Telecom and Bell Canada, and is an advisor to Thomas F. Hill Associates, a communications consulting firm.

Prior to establishing his own research and consulting business, Mr. Strauss spent nine years with a Fortune 500 company, where he was involved in product management, corporate planning and the development of international operations.

He is a graduate of Yale University and attended the New York University Graduate School of Business Administration, where he majored in finance.